Prepare for the Worst and Pray for the Best

"A Layman's Guide to Surviving a Nation gone Bad"

Ronald A. Martin Jr.

DEDICATION

I dedicate this book to my family, friends, and God. Without your support and belief in me this book would not have become a reality. I cannot forget my brothers and sisters in the armed forces, without your faithful and dedicated service none of us would be enjoying our freedoms. God Bless you all!

CONTENTS

Prepare for the Worst and Pray for the best

"Invest and save aggressively but enjoy life, live below your means but don't hold back on the ones you love. Smile and lend a hand to those in need. Prepare for the worse and pray for the best"
-Ronald Martin

"You can have it all, just not all at once."
-Oprah Winfrey

"The best way to get what you want in life is to deserve what you want."
-Charlie Munger

Preface

I'm not famous, I'm not affluent, I'm not racist, nor am I crazy. I have been called an extremist before and that is alright by me, because to me an extremist is someone who loves his country very much, but also prepares him/herself for the possible wrongs that can happen to us all. But really I'm a normal God fearing, American patriot who loves his country and family. I have seen and read a lot of books of late about the turmoil our country is in. Issues such as the economy, immigration, unemployment, welfare/entitlements, and politics and religion have had many articles, pamphlets, and books written about each topic in great detail.

I don't want to repeat the same information and seem like I'm beating a dead-horse, but I feel that these issues and many more like them have to be analyzed and discussed from many different perspectives and point of views to reach as many Americans as possible. I don't want to just talk about the problems plaguing this country, but offer some solutions to the layman (the common person) of how to adjust, adapt, and overcome them. I started tracking the "Great Recession" in late 2007 purely out of curiosity.

The more research I conducted the more curious and depressed I became. I didn't actually decide to write a book until mid-2010 when my notes started to fill with interesting facts and events that were taking place in the world and especially in this country. These events woke me up, so I decided to try my luck in awakening as many Americans as I could.

Most of us are so busy with our daily lives and trying to make ends meet, we get lost in all that happens outside our little circles. The media keeps our minds boggled with nonsense such as Charlie Sheen and Lindsey Lohan's latest shenanigans without mentioning the ongoing crisis in the Middle East, our borders being invaded, and our economy continuously staying in the crapper.

This once great nation has fallen, and it is up to each and every one of us to lift her back up to prominence again. On the plus side, those of us who survive our countries transition will re-learn what most people outside of small towns have forgotten- - the necessity of God, family, friends, and community. The necessary sacrifice and humility we now must face. I'm no different than anyone else and the events that woke me up and made me start paying attention should definitely do the same for you.

Knowledge is most definitely power, whether you get it in a classroom, internet, or books makes no difference. I will also take you on an eye opening journey that will hopefully provide you with some insight, advice, and secrets on what is going on in this country and what may happened to the millions of Americans that are oblivious to what is going on around them.

The information in this book will teach you (the layman), how to prepare yourself for the worst and the importance of praying not just for the best but for our country that was indeed founded on religion. As the title says a "layman's guide to surviving a nation gone bad", I will provide numerous checklists that will guide you through the process of preparing for the worst and surviving the best way we know how to. At the end of each chapter I will include a very interesting section called "*We the People have spoken*", taken from blogs, radio and television shows, and just talking to people on how they actually feel about what they see is happening to our once great country. Some are funny and some are shocking truths, so read on and enjoy.

Introduction

I grew up in North Carolina in the late 70's and 80's as what I like to call myself an "Asian Redneck." My Mother was born in Burma and became a United States Citizen in 1968, and my Father was born and raised in Tennessee. My family was lower middle class at best with little to no education beyond a high school diploma or GED, but times were much easier then. Both my parents had good strong work ethics, strong morals, and were frugal; all these traits would filter down to me and my brother over time. I also grew up in the age of discipline and consequences, something almost unheard of in today's society. Today, it is common for your kids to call the police on you if you hit/discipline them. Lord knows we need to bring that back or it will be lost forever.

Today's high-income and high consumption life style has Americans living for today, not looking towards the future, and losing sight of everything this country was founded on. I would love to be able to turn the clock back when people were content and happy with what they had, neighbors helping one another out, and we didn't have to worry about locking our doors at night. No one had any savings outside the few fortunate that were financially able to prepare for retirement. One income was all it took to partake in the American Dream, which at that time was owning a basic house and one car, while the other parent (usually the mother) spent quality time with the kids, ensuring that they were getting a proper upbringing.

Higher education was something that the more privileged pursued and a high school diploma and a good work ethic got the rest of us a respectable job to where we could support our family and make a decent living. Unlike today when waving at someone might get you shot, people were friendly and went out of their way to help each other. I had no immediate desire to pursue a college degree, due to the fact that my grades were poor and my family did not have the money to even fathom paying for any college. So needless to say when I graduated High School in June 1986 (by the skin of my teeth), college was not on my list of things to do. At the time I had no clue what I was going to do with my life other than work and get by like everyone else around me was doing. But then my girlfriend got pregnant and we had a baby boy in December of 1986. That changed things dramatically for me. Now I had to not only think about taking care of myself, but a family as well. We got married in January 1987 and I joined the United States Navy five days later that same month and year.

I have never been one to shy away from hard work. As a matter of fact it is one of the main foundations that this Country was built on. I started out with a paper route at the age of twelve years old. On the weekends I would help out at a local farm cleaning horse stables and stacking hay. When I turned fifteen I started working at a car wash, and from the ages of sixteen until eighteen I did construction work as a roofer, brick layer, and an electrician's helper. It seemed normal back then to start working at a young age and continue to work hard for everything that you had or will have. At least I had the luxury to finish school and not have to drop-out of school to help support my family like my father and uncle had to do before me.

Nothing was handed out. You worked hard academically and mentally if you wanted to go to college, you worked hard physically if you wanted that decent paying job down the street, and you may have had to combine all three if you wanted anything outside of the norm. But it made you feel good about yourself and you slept well at night, knowing that you worked hard for everything that you had. It also helped you develop a strong work ethic that would help carry you through the good and bad times that we will all face.

Joining the Navy was without a doubt the best decision I have ever made in my life. I mean the economy in those days was pretty darn good and the cost of living in North Carolina was even better. I came in the Navy as a Radioman because my ASVAB scores were not high enough to get the jobs I really wanted (lack of education). The first few years were very tough, the money I was getting paid qualified me and my family for WIC and just barely kept us above the poverty line. We had our second child (my daughter) in Nov of 1989 and life got a little (financially) tougher. I was lucky enough to make E-5 off the March 1991 exam cycle, I made a little more money but with the lack of education, desire, and drive I stayed stuck there as if time had frozen for me for almost ten years. In 1998 the Radioman rate and the Data Processors combined into one rate called Information Systems Technicians (IT). That may have been the turning point for me as I finally made E-6 and started learning a job skill that would take the world by storm.

I also got to see the world, where I have been to and saw more countries than I have states. I have seen some extraordinary places in my twenty two years, but I have also seen some bad places. If you have never been to a third world country consider yourself lucky. It was definitely an eye opening experience and I got to see first-hand how bad it really is out there. It also made me appreciate where I lived and how good I have it compared to others. If we don't do everything we can and work together, third world country status may not be that far off for us all and trust me we don't want that.

As I was continuing to work hard and living the American dream, things around me were changing. The new generation, "GenYers" as I like to call them was getting lazy, complacent, and the world was letting them get away with it. I can honestly say that I was one of the many Americans that were oblivious to what was going on around me. I had a house, a couple of cars, two kids, and a wife. What I did not realize was the increasing debt that was surrounding my life. My current wife and I were both wreck less with our finances. I had no clue what I owed on my house or what my interest rate was. I had two cars at that time and I'm sure my interest rate was high especially since I was a young sailor in a military town.

Things got tougher for us in those early years, as we were running up debt, bouncing checks, and falling behind on almost every bill we had, my check went into the bank and came out next to nothing. I had my car repossessed, foreclosed on my first house all at the age of twenty one years old. That is when I began to wake up financially. I made a promise to myself that I would recover and never put myself in that situation again. That is also when I started to teach myself financial responsibility. I found ways to pay off my bills without filing for bankruptcy, I found ways to cut-back (life within my means) as much as I could to get ahead and I found ways to start saving money. I was a late bloomer in that area, but just as in life, it's better late than never.

This country was founded on religion. The founding fathers knew it was important to lay a solid foundation built on religion for citizens to apply to their everyday life and the Bible was the perfect guideline to govern a country by. My family was not big church goers during my childhood, but religion was a big part of their early lives and they made sure we knew about God. I started attending a Church of God with my friends as a teenager and became a Christian at the age of fifteen. My mother also gave her life to Christ around that time. God has always been a big part of my life and I continue to give him the glory for all good things that happen in my life.

My military career also kept me close to God, because if it were not for my personal relationship with him, I would not have made it through 22 years. I have tried to instill the Christian ways in my family and friends, by always trying to do the right thing and help my fellow man as much as I could. I am not a bible toting street preacher, but I do mentor to those who I feel need it and try to let God shine in my life through my daily actions.

As I take a look at the current condition of this once great nation I see that religion is fading. It has been taken out of schools, taken out of the work place, talked about taken off our currency, and new man-made religions have been created. Now you have to be politically correct and say holiday party instead of Christmas party. The Catholics even recently change the seven deadly sins (probably to cater to their following). In recent decades, the wealthy have become more educated, more metropolitan-based, and less religious. It seems as though our religious leaders are more concerned about catering to people by telling them what they want to hear than preaching the word of God. If you don't know the word of God, I caution you of the many heretics that are out there like wolves in sheep's clothing (does the name Harold Camping ring a bell?). The same goes for politics, if you don't know the issues, the candidates, and who they are and what they stand for, you will be led astray. I cannot stress enough how important knowledge is. If you don't educate yourself, you will be educated by society and the school of hard knocks.

Politically this country has pretty much always been split in half, red (republican) and blue (democrat). Few of us want to pay more taxes; few of us want to give up services, benefits and entitlements that the government provides. No one wants a police state; no one wants anarchy. We want to eat, drink, sleep, work, travel, and love freely and safely. No one wants to be left in a ditch to die like a dog. But we as Americans are at the crossroads, and simply doing nothing is all it will take for our great nation to go down the toilet. The great American patriot and Founding Father Thomas Jefferson once said that *"All Tyranny needs to gain a foothold is for people of good conscience to remain silent."*

The last five years of my military career turned out to be the defining part of my life. I was promoted to E-7(Chief), got my Bachelor's degree in Business Management, finished off six project management certifications, and retired with a desirable job skill. I started to pay closer attention to the things that were happening around me financially, politically, and religiously. I became a NRA certified instructor in the pistol and home defense disciplines after retiring from the military, to be able to teach my family and friends the importance of gun safety and knowing how to shoot and protect themselves. I also started to take self-defense classes and began studying Muay-Thai. I keep these tools fined tuned and try to prepare myself for any situation that may come my way.

You will read more in depth about what I'm talking about in the coming chapters. No American citizen should be judged by the color of his or her skin, by his or her appearance, nor by his or her ethnic background or cultural beliefs. This book will show you the small steps I took to finally get and stay ahead. It will tell you how to notice the tell-tale signs of a Nation going bad and what you can do to prepare yourself. Because let's face it most of us that are hardworking, law-abiding, and children raising Americans do not have the time to pay attention to what is going on in the world, watch the news or surf the internet all-day long. We just know it isn't right.

This book is based upon how a normal hardworking American citizen that considers himself to be a gun toting, NRA lifetime member, Christian conservative that came from next to nothing, overcame adversity, scrutiny, racism, and many other obstacles that confronted him and turned his life around for the better. Life is a continuing journey and education is always the key to being successful.

I

Higher Education (What does it means to you)

"There are three ingredients in the good life: learning, earning, and yearning."
-Christopher Morely
"Knowledge will be the key resource of the Next Society...Knowledge workers will be the dominant group in the workforce."
-Peter Drucker

I can only tell you and try to relate to you what higher education meant and means to me. I was fortunate enough to realize early that life doesn't come to you no matter how long you wait. As a matter of fact if you wait long enough you will be alone, broke, and sixty –something wondering what the hell happened. You have to go out get what you want and what you think you deserve. If you believe you don't deserve anything and your fine with your life passing you by, then simply do nothing.

If you're one of the millions out there expecting and wanting the government to take care of you, then maybe this book isn't for you. But if you have the drive, the work-ethic, and the will to be successful then maybe you can pick up a few things from this book that will help you achieve the things you want in life. It all starts with education.

Now I know there are a few self-made millionaires out there that made it without a college degree and some without a high school diploma, but they educated themselves about something and that was the foundation of their success. There are no longer such things as safe jobs or stable careers anymore. The grueling economy over the last several years has put an end to that pipe dream. But Americans with a college degree are making out better than the folks without one. Some people say that education is life and without it you will walk around this country like a zombie (I like that word).

In a recent Gallup Poll, Americans say a good education is what matters most to getting ahead in life today. Hard work comes in right behind it. In fact, it may be difficult to have one without the other. Most of us do not have the luxury of just going to school to get a degree. We have to work, take care of the kids and the house, and then find extra time to attend school anyway we can get it by sacrificing sleep and many other extracurricular activities to try and make our lives better. I will say that with the advance of technology it is easier to accomplish this task.

Others say education means freedom from poverty and freedom from stereotypes. Higher education helps people to see the world in rational ways for the benefit of all. It helps eliminate ignorance and several myths plaguing the world. Educated people get wider vision to perceive the facts of the life.

Knowledge gives us the power to do what we want to do. There was a time in history when the privileged elite (educated) used the power of knowledge to control people, and in some cases around this country they still do. Education is not an end in itself but a means to leading a productive life and career. Education is a way out. Period. Ted Nugent in his book "Ted, White, and Blue" said that "Education is not a white value to be shunned and mocked, but a human value to be embraced, cherished, and passed on to future generations".

17

If we are the most powerful, technologically advanced nation on earth, then why are there over 32 million Americans who cannot read or write? I mean I know that this is not a nation of law or finance scholars, but according to the Department of Education and the studies that they have conducted over the years revealed that nearly two-thirds of the respondents struggled to make sense of a bus schedule, and half could not add two items on a lunch menu and calculate a 10% tip. Sixty-three percent of ages 18 – 24 could not locate Iraq on a map, seventy percent shrugged their shoulders when asked where Iran and Israel were, and ninety-nine percent had no clue where Afghanistan was. What is being taught in school these days? America needs engineers, scientists, computer specialists, entrepreneurs, and all other professional specialties that require a college education. To ignore educations is to spit on that for which our forefathers worked so hard for.

To make things worse a 2003 study by a Yale University researcher revealed that more than 50% of first year college students could not produce papers free of grammatical errors, and eighty percent of graduating college seniors say they will never again voluntarily read another book. Only one-third of U.S. students are proficient readers; two-thirds lack sufficient reading ability to comprehend novels, textbooks, this book, and other forms of complicated writing. Democracy requires an educated middle class for its survival, and requires citizens to vote for the country's leaders and policies. It's pretty simple, if you can't read the ballot, understand the positional argument the candidates are making, if you don't know the history of this country and our laws how can you decide who to vote for? Why do we take our opportunities and college experience for granted?

Median real earnings for American workers lacking a college degree have stagnated or declined since 1974 as incomes of the most affluent Americans have soared. Let me throw out some figures that should stick in your head. One in four from the age of 25 or older has obtained a Bachelor's degree. The average annual salary from those lucky enough to achieve this goal is about $46.8k per year. That sure does beat the salary of the 43.6 million Americans living in poverty as of 2009. Oh yeah by the way the poverty line is a family of four making less than $22,000 dollars (all sources of income) a year or an individual making less than $11,000 a year. Another figure that should wake you up is the unemployment rate among workers with college degrees is 4.5%, where high school graduates with no college is 10.1%, and amongst high school dropouts are 13.8 %.(See figure 1 for more information on these statistics). So that stat shows the more education you have the better off you are.

I'm not saying that once you get your degree life as you know it is automatically better or will shower you with guaranteed riches, but your almost guaranteed not to become insolvent despite the rising costs of a college education. While pursuing a college degree is definitely the way to go a whopping 85% of college seniors had to move back home after graduation in May 2010. While getting your degree use to be viewed as a stepping stone to limitless career opportunities, college graduates are now reduced to living under their parents or a well-to-do relative's roof. You can blame most of it on the current condition of the economy (which will be discussed further in chapter two) and the high unemployment rate that still plagues our nation today.

BOB ENGLEHART, COPYRIGHT 2010 CAGLE CARTOONS

Education also plays an important role in the job market, even in difficult times. Companies are hiring and always have been, but they are being very selective in their hiring process. They are looking for skilled workers with the right qualifications and the truth of the matter is there aren't that many qualified folks out there looking for jobs. Another survey conducted by Towers Watson, a human resources consulting firm says as the economy is picking up (I still don't see it), employers are having a harder time attracting and retaining skilled employees.

More than half the companies surveyed said they've had difficulty attracting and finding critical-skilled employees. While companies are confident enough to give raises, they are still cautious when it comes to hiring. I have changed jobs three times in three years during the recession because I wanted to, not because I had to. When immigrants illegal and legal are filling the void on most blue collar jobs, you have to set yourself apart to qualify for white collar jobs. The best way to accomplish this is more education. You have to get in the habit of always finding ways to build your worth to a current or prospective employer. Whether it is by staying connected and updated on the current issues in your field, or taking an additional course or two to make yourself more flexible and thus more valuable in your filed and to your employer. You should never sit around and let the grass grow under your feet. A wise man once told me that the best time to look for a job is when you have a job.

Degrees are necessary in certain high-income jobs such as physicians, attorneys, dentist, accountants, engineers, architects, veterinarians, information systems professionals, and chiropractors. What do these professionals sell? What they sell most of all is their intellect. These professional are also very portable, because they use and are paid for their intellect/knowledge, they do not have a high-cost overhead. So if you are preparing to go to college and looking for a profitable degree, don't sleep on the ones I just mentioned.

Most Valuable Degrees

What makes a college degree valuable?
- Career opportunities
- Starting compensation
- Time to completion
- Versatility

Here is a list of the most valuable degrees based on the above criteria.

1. Bachelor's Degree in Business – This is the most popular college degree in the world and it is also the best college degree.
   Time to completion: 4 years
   Starting income: $41,100
   Mid – career income: $70,600
   Winning Factor: One of the advantages of a business degree is that you are able to move into many different industries.

2. Associate's Degree in Medical Assisting – The timing for earning this degree could not be better. The suddenly red-

hot career was high-lighted in Laurence Shatkin's book "Best Jobs for the 21st Century" and was also named by Forbes as one of the fastest growing jobs for women in 2010.

Time to completion: 2 years

Average income: $29,450

Potential income: $39,970

Winning Factor: Medical assisting opportunities are expected to grow an amazing 34% between 2010 and 2018, according to the U.S. Dept. of Labor.

3. Bachelor's Degree in Accounting – Accounting is often overshadowed by the more popular business degree but the income figures are higher for this more specialized degree.

Time to completion: 4 years

Starting income: $46,500

Mid – career income: $77,500

Winning Factor: There are a lot of opportunities for those with this degree, In a recent survey of more than 500 senior finance executives, more than half of the CFOs expressed concern about a lack of qualified accountants entering the workforce.

4. Associate's Degree in Paralegal Studies – It's hard to find a two-year degree with more upside. This extremely solid degree allows you to work for a law firm or for yourself, in whatever city or town you want in America. And the pay is great.

Time to completion: 2 years

Average income: $50,080

Potential income: $75,700

Winning Factor: Opportunities for paralegals and legal assistants are expected to grow at a healthy 28% between 2010 and 2018, according to the U.S. Dept. of Labor.

5. Bachelors of Science in Nursing – Add security to the long list of reason's to become a nurse. A Vanderbilt University analysis in 2009 predicted that the U.S. will have a shortage of 260,000 nurses in 2025.

Time to completion: 4 years

Starting income: $52,700

Mid – career income: $68,200

Winning Factor: Employment opportunities are expected to soar 22% between 2010 and 2018, with hundreds of thousands of job openings expected from retirements, according to the U.S. Dept. of Labor.

With that in mind you may view a college degree as no more than a 150k – 250k dollar piece of paper. In today's brave new world you have to combine your college experience with a valuable job skill and that may mean starting at the bottom at a lesser salary than you want or possibly relocating to a more lucrative state. Considering that the unemployment rate for ages 20 – 24 is 15% that may not be such a bad thing (See Figure 1). That is why I preach joining the military to today's youth. You can learn a valuable job skill that you work in on a day-to-day basis and earn a degree that the military pays for. When and if you decide to get out you have both the degree and the on-the-job-training that employers are looking for.

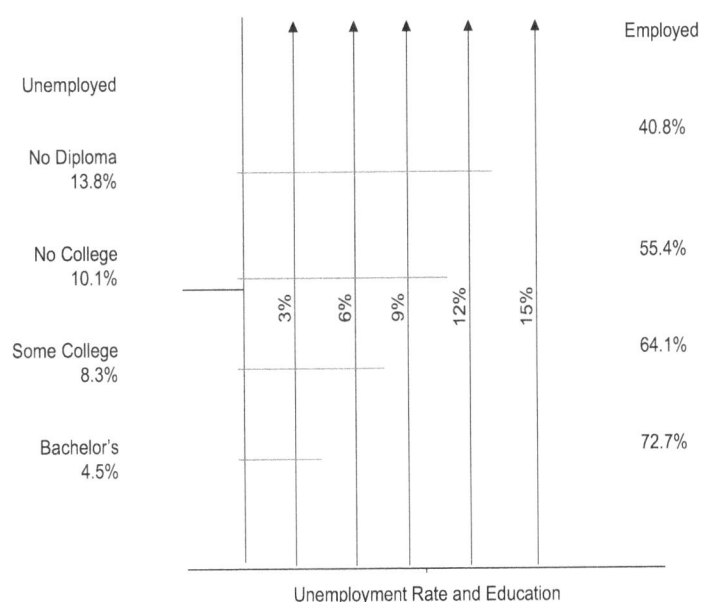

Unemployment Rate and Education

Figure 1

The only problem now is that it isn't as easy to get into the military as it once was. The military is only accepting high school seniors before they graduate so they can get them on the delayed entry program. Once you graduate, you have to join the reserve program and continue to put in requests to go active duty. Don't get me wrong the reserves is also a great place to be as you will qualify for the new G.I. bill and begin to earn your degree there. Today's youth are so misguided nowadays and most are not even considering the military as an option in this horrible economy.

The school aged children in America seemed to be almost scripted and guided through the system. Teachers and faculty do not want to hurt the child's feelings or make them feel inadequate about not performing up to par. You hardly hear of a child failing a grade nowadays, they just get pushed through the system feeling special and with the mind-set that the world owes them something. Even on the sports field there is no winners or losers in today's world. That doesn't make sense in my mind, because in the real world there are winners and losers, we need competition in our lives to drive us to become better at what we want to do.

I have several school aged children still in my household from the second grade on up to community college. It seems that none of them know much about the history of this country. You can ask them to name three of the Founding fathers of our great country and you get a blank stare and a list of names such as Abraham Lincoln and Paul Revere to go along with George Washington. They just don't have a clue because they are not being taught any of this. They are being taught that they deserve this and that and the resources in this country are theirs for the taking. They are being taught that they can have it all without working for any of it. So they still leave the ultimate responsibility on the parents to teach their children about the history of this country and how only hard work, sacrifice, and a good work ethic will get you the things that you want. If you think that I'm wrong just ask your children when they get home from school each day what did you learn.

Let's take a brief look at how children in America take for granted privileges such as going to school and receiving a decent education and what it looks like in a third world country. When we battle issues such as making sure our children wake-up in time for school so they won't miss too many days or listen to them tell us that the teacher is mean, they have no clue what other children around the world would give to take their place. Let's also note that there are more than 100 million children worldwide that do not attend school for one reason or another.

A normal village school in Pakistan consists of about 100 children from all different ages sitting on a crowded mud floor. The only furniture in the room is a table and a chair for the teacher. It is raining outside and the classroom is cold and sticky. The children shiver with cold, but have learned how to sit still and be quiet. The teacher reads from a book, and the children repeat what he/she says. Due to lack of funding most third world countries offer poor quality programs, taught by poorly qualified teachers, that you guessed it are paid poorly if at all. Lack of school supplies, resources, and yes the internet make teaching and learning a living nightmare.

Can you imagine the impact of having the ability to teach third world youths the needed skills to become a researcher, a doctor, or even the philosophy and ideas behind freedom and democracy? Due to language problems, poverty, unbearable school conditions, a child's inability to follow the teacher, and many, many more reasons that attribute to the high drop-out rate in these third world countries have become a trauma for many children as well as their parents and teachers. It is an assault on their very humanity.

In countries such as El Salvador many public schools were not rebuilt after the earthquake and long civil war. In Soweto/South Africa only one third of the students were able to be enrolled due to social and political unrest. In Kinshasa, many school girls would change their clothes from their school uniform to a dress right after class and sell their body in order to get a warm meal. But school remains a dream linked to a better life and living conditions for these children. They remain optimistic and believe the experience school provides is worth the trouble.

I started working towards my Bachelors of Science in Management in October 2003 onboard a Navy ship. There were many times when I felt like giving up and not completing my degree program. I was trying to accomplish my schooling while performing my daily duties as the leading petty officer onboard my ship, a father of two kids, and about a hundred or more other excuses that surrounded me at the time.

There were times I had to put school off for a month or two at a time because of the work load of the ship. But I kept my eye on the prize and I knew that it would better my life and my family's life one day soon, if and when I completed it. In March 2005 I finally transferred off the ship to Space and Naval Warfare Systems Center Norfolk (SPAWARSYSCEN). That transition made things a lot easier for me as my life finally started to settle down again except I was going through a divorce after twenty years of marriage. The point I'm trying to make here is that life will keep throwing curve balls at you, but you have to keep pushing. I am a goal oriented person, so when I made finishing my degree my short term goal, there was not much that could stop me at that point. When I finally finished in October 2007 I had about eight months left until retirement from the United States Navy after almost 22 years.

When I finished my degree I immediately started working on my certifications in project management. Higher education and learning become like a drug, once you get started (which is the hardest part), you don't want to stop. I was lucky enough to have the military pay for almost all of my education, but there are many avenues out there that make obtaining a college degree possible for just about anyone. It is not easy and I will not try to make it sound like it is, but with hard work, persistence, and the drive to succeed you will have all the tools you need. It immediately became one of the highlights of my life. Now after being out of the military for almost three years, I began to realize the importance of my accomplishment and the many opportunities it presented me.

Now that I have talked about the importance of us being educated in many realms and not just school, we have to become educators. We have to not only do our homework on the daily goings on in our country, but we have to convey our knowledge and thoughts to our families, neighbors, co-workers, and whoever else wants and needs to hear it. With education you can learn to use a pen like a word (the media does it all the time), write with such conviction that you can persuade millions of people to hear your message, and learn and use technology to continuously get the word out. I truly feel this is the only way we can fight this battle to win our country back.

The Art of Resume Writing

I'm not a scholar so I cannot and will not write numerous pages on this subject, but I will include other topics that I feel belong in this chapter that will help you succeed in a very competitive job market where successful resume writing is one of them. The importance of this ability is priceless, having been on both ends of submitting and reviewing resumes I believe I can provide you with enough insight on how to do this without spending hundreds of dollars.

Many people think that a resume is only for white collar jobs. In our ever-changing job market everyone will need a resume, including blue collar workers. The resume is a selling tool that outlines your skills and experiences so an employer can see, at a glance, how you can contribute to the employer's workplace. The goal of an effective resume is to highlight and summarize a person's qualifications. You should have a few different versions of your resume ready to go at any moment. First you should have the one page resume hitting all the main points and tailored to the job you are applying for. In some cases hiring managers are too busy to read a four or five page resume and anything over one may get tossed in the trash or filed away. Here is an example of an IT professional applying for a systems administrator job with a security clearance.

JOHN A. DOE JR.

ADDRESS, EMAIL, PHONE #

OBJECTIVE

Information Systems Technician with a background in Network Management and System Administration in GOTS Delta, WIN2K, WIN2K3, XP, Compose 2&3, and UNIX.

SECURITY CLEARANCE

Active TS/SCI clearance based on a Single Scope Background Investigation (SSBI).

CAREER HIGHLIGHTS

Information Technology Specialist with specialized training and experience in Network Management and Systems Administration.

Skilled and experienced in problem-solving and decision-making in high- tempo, Time-critical environments. Unparalleled communication and organizational skills as a direct result of extensive experience in managing planning, and executing a broad range of communications operations in support of contingencies and operational planning. Experienced in managing a multitude of tasks simultaneously, solving complex problems, and arriving at effective solutions Dynamic, innovative professional with superior leadership qualities and successful team- building experience.

EDUCATION

- International Correspondence Schools, Diploma: Fitness and Nutrition
- University of Phoenix Online Student, Associates of Arts in General Studies 4/2006
- University of Phoenix Online Student, Bachelors of Science in

Management 11/2007

- University of Phoenix Online Student, Project Management
  Certification - Ongoing

COMPUTER SKILLS

Microsoft Office; Microsoft Windows; GOTS Delta, Compose 2&3, and UNIX

Cisco Routers and Switches General Networking Wireless Networking Skills

CETIFICATIONS FROM TECHNICAL SCHOOLS

High Frequency Surface Communication System Operator 12/1995

Super High Frequency SATCOM Training 6/1996

CCNA 7/2000

Radio Operator 4/2002

Network/Computer Systems Administrator 2/2006

In the objective column is where you want to take the job description of the job you're applying for and insert the keywords such as system administrator that is proficient in various operating systems with a minimum secret security clearance. I'm not telling you to lie on your resume, because you will be expected to know the information that is in your resume. But if you have done a job that is very similar to the one you are applying for or have some general knowledge of what they are asking for then tailor your resume to read as such.

The rest of your resume must convince the hiring authority that you have the background and skills to do the job and are well worth an interview. Some tips to follow are to make sure you spell check your resume and have a few people look it over. The person hiring will use your resume as the first impression stage. If you have an email address such as bigdaddy69@hotmail.com then change it to your first dot last name (john.doe@hotmail.com). It looks more professional and your resume will be easier to locate if they want to review it again. Next you do want to have the four or five page resume in your possession and ready to submit if the employer asks for more information on you.

Your resume should be a living document. What I mean by that is you should always be finding ways to improve yourself and add these improvements to your resume. There are many free classes and seminars given at your local library that relate to many various topics such as basic computer knowledge. You can and should add these to your resume. Make sure that it is always up to date and that you have several copies in your possession. Now that we have a resume template established, submitting it to the right places should be your next step. Sites such as monster.com, usajobs.gov, securejobs.com, theladders.com are free of charge and great places to submit your resume.

Also just going directly to the company and submitting your resume is also a good idea. Do not overlook going to job fairs either. If nothing else it is another place to submit your resume. Do not make yourself feel that you are too inexperienced or do not have enough information to put in a resume. I helped my kids when they were eighteen years old write a resume that were at least good enough to be looked at. That is all you can hope for in today's job market. The more it gets looked at, the more chance you have to land a job. Here is a checklist to help guide you on your path to success.

Checklist for Success

Get Educated – Use resources available to you. If you need assistance start applying for it now. There are tons of scholarships and grants available to you, just search the internet. But you should not rely on anyone but yourself when it comes to your education. Educating yourself does not have to be college course either. You can keep yourself up-to-date on current events, reading books or magazines, and conducting your own research on various issue that surround us today.

Build an effective Resume – Read *The Art of Resume Writing in* Chapter 1. And get it out to as many people and businesses as you can.

Interview – A successful interview begins with homework and preparation. Research the company. Plan and prepare for interview questions and practice your answers to common questions. Know your strengths and weaknesses. Dress for success and be confident. **Stage one** (Introductory stage): The interviewer forms an initial impression that can contribute to acceptance or rejection. The decision to hire is not made at this stage, but it begins here. Remember, you never get a second chance to make a first impression! **Stage two** (Employer Questions): The interviewer tries to determine how well your attitude and skills fit with the company image and work culture. The interviewer is trying to match your specific skills and abilities to the job. **Stage three** (Applicant questions): The interviewer is trying to determine your level of interest in the job and your degree of knowledge about the company. This is the time to clear up uncertainties. **Stage four** (Closing stage): The interviewer will draw the session to a close. If you want the job, make your intentions clear now. Follow up after the interviews, send thank you notes or a letter to the interviewer. If you do not get the job, analyze why. Rejections are part of the process and you should not get discouraged or take it personally. Just start preparing for the next one.

Continue to Educate yourself – enough said.

Stay positive and engaged – Don't let the grass grow under your feet. Most people give up after a few rejections. But remember we are living in a different day and age and you have to go above and beyond to be successful.

Blogs in relation to this Chapter (We the People have Spoken)

- *If we don't have homes to go to, what good is an education?*

- *I have a Bachelor's Degree in accounting and finance. For people with BA's who can't find jobs, the main reasons are: lack of internships, low GPA, bad resumes, or low demanding majors like music education.*

- *I'm 60. I've heard since college that my children's generation will not have it as good as my parents had it. Here's some news, my generation (in retirement) won't have it as good as my parents had it in their retirement. My kid's generation will be worse, and my grandchildren's generation may possibly see third world country status by then. We owe a great deal of thanks to our corrupt, incompetent, spend thrift government. History books will show that the last 40 years of government was what destroyed the very fiber of this once great country.*

- *Hard work is much more important than an education at this point. A college degree won't feed a family.*

- *People with college degrees that were laid off have found new employment while those with high school diplomas are still struggling.*

- *The American Dream has become working two jobs in a small apartment, I'm sure glad I went to college, otherwise I wouldn't have been able to get these two horrible jobs three years after graduating.*

II

State of the economy

(Tracking the "Great Recession")

Suffering isn't ennobling, recovery is.
-Christian Barnard

This topic alone could be a title of a book and filled with hundreds of pages. I'm not going to go there because I'm not that smart and I don't think like an economist. But I will tell you in layman terms what I think you want to know and what I think you need to know and yes, this chapter will be a doozie.....

This country has been in three known depressions. The first documented one was 1837, followed by the depression of 1893. The one we have all heard about is the Great Depression of 1929. This was the granddaddy of them all and it affected the entire globe. The stock market crashed (known as black Tuesday), half of the 25,000 banks failed, and unemployment rose to 25%. Kind of sounds familiar doesn't it? But this one lasted over ten years and the effects of it are still being felt. Below I will list all the Post World War II recessions this country has faced:

Start – End	Duration
Nov 1948 – Oct 1949	11 months
July 1953 – May 1954	10 months
Aug 1957 – Apr 1958	8 months
Apr 1960 – Feb 1961	10 months
Dec 1969 – Nov 1970	11 months
Nov 1973 – Mar 1975	16 months
Jan 1980 – July 1980	6 months
July 1981 – Nov 1982	16 months
July 1990 – Mar 1991	8 months
Mar 2001 – Nov 2001	8 months
Dec 2007 – Jun 2009	18 months

Noting that the last one has been the longest recession this country has suffered through since the "Great Depression". The funny thing at the writing of this book is that not one of us believes that the "Great Recession" has ended. (1) It took fifteen months for the National Bureau of Economic Research (NBER) to conduct the research and make the announcement. NBER said that June 2009 was the point where the economy stopped falling and began to rise. No matter how small that rise was, that stat brought us out of recession.

Ordinarily news of this magnitude on a recession that lasted this long would boost consumer spirits, but even the economists seemed mystified by a "recovery" characterized by sky-high unemployment (nearly 10%), falling incomes, record poverty, and an endless stream of home foreclosures. (2) The rising phase has nearly stopped rising. Companies have stopped the massive layoffs, but are barely hiring. NBER's pronouncement means that if the economy slips back into recession, it will officially be back-to-back recessions, not a prolonged or double dip recession. When the unemployed begin to find work, home values stabilize or begin to rise, consumers start spending, and the government stops stimulating, that will then signal an end to the nation's psychological recession. (3) Since June 2009, jobs in twenty seven states got worse.

Even though the nation's unemployment rate remained at 9.7%, Nevada, Michigan, and California were up above 12%. And thirteen other states were up over 10% as of August 2010. The real truth my friends is that this may be the new norm.

How can the government manipulate the numbers on paper to pull us out of recession and raise the GDP? The government accounts for 30% of the Nations income. So how can by transferring dollars from account-to-account boost the GDP by a tenth of a percent to allegedly pull us out of recession. That is what our economist agreed on, but believe me not a single soul I know celebrated. The usual signs that bring a decisive end to recessions — such as demand for housing, spike in consumer spending, and job hiring have yet to materialize at the writing of this book. And without these things, it leaves the country wide open for another recession that is likely looming over the horizon.

There was a rumor circulating back in 1994 that a working group was put together in the 80's, months after the 1987 stock market crash. This working group was comprised of some pretty big hitters such as the secretary of treasury and the chairman of the Federal Reserve Board along with some other stock market chief executives later to be known as the Plunge Protection Team (PPT). The purpose the PPT was to enhance the integrity, efficiency, orderliness, and competitiveness of the financial markets and maintain investor's confidence. They set up something of a war room, maintained a global as well as a national list of key contacts, and carried out simulated emergency drills. Just how much power did the PPT have and was allowed to use was never made clear. A year after retiring from the Fed's board, Robert Hiller wrote, that instead of flooding the entire economy with liquidity, and thereby increasing the danger of inflation, the Fed could support the stock market directly by buying market averages in the futures market, thus stabilizing the market as a whole.

It was also reported that the Fed could theoretically buy anything to pump money into the system. That included state and local debt, real estate, and gold mines. There is belief that this team represents a powerful and secretive hand that is ready to act any time the Dow or the country looks ready to tank.

Let's take a look at the unemployment picture of the last several years and at the writing of this book. The population of this country is right around 311 million people and the nationwide average of unemployment is 9.6%. As of late 2010 there were approximately 16 million people unemployed, 9 million under employed, and 4 million are barely working or are so discouraged that they have given up looking for jobs. This picture does not reflect the true numbers because several million people are not qualified for unemployment. A reliable source said that the true unemployment rate is right around 21%.

There are roughly 140 million Americans still working, that is less than half our population. At the current rate of job creation, the nation would need at least nine years to recover all the lost jobs during the recession, not to include the five or six million jobs that will be needed in that span of time to keep pace with our expanding population. Here is just a peak of how bad things really are. This is the unemployment numbers from the numbers guru.com over the last twenty years:

1990	5.3%	2000	4.0%
1991	6.8%	2001	4.7%
1992	7.5%	2002	5.8%
1993	6.9%	2003	6.0%
1994	6.1%	2004	5.5%
1995	5.6%	2005	5.1%

1996	5.4%	2006	4.6%
1997	4.9%	2007	4.6%
1998	6.1%	2008	5.8%
1999	4.2%	2009	9.3%
2010	9.7%	2011	9.0%

The unemployment of 2009 and 2010 has been by far the highest over the last twenty years. John Williams, founder of Shadow Government Statistics, says when accounting for the long-term unemployed, the jobless rate runs up to as high as 22% currently. The worse unemployment got during the "Great Depression" was 25% and that is scary. The unemployed have collected a total of $319 billion dollars in jobless benefits over the last three years. Since the "stimulus bill" was passed the unemployment benefits have been extended out to ninety- nine weeks from sixty- five weeks those numbers will continue to grow. Those 11 million people that are receiving jobless benefits are frequently called the 99ers.

And guess what? The millions of people who could not find a job in those ninety nine weeks (almost 2 years) want another extension. That is what I call insanity. I mean the Federal government has spent $156 billion dollars in jobless benefits in 2010 alone. Forty million dollars per day is being paid out in unemployment benefits by the federal government (tax payers/workers). What these people (99ers) don't realize is that the longer you stay unemployed the more difficult it will be to re-enter the labor force, because they lose skills and employers question their suitability for employment. It is also hampering the economy because the jobless households are reluctant to spend due to uncertainties of future income.

It's obvious that Americans view unemployment much more urgently than the law makers, congress, and even the president does. This scenario will lead me into my next topic of welfare benefits in America. In the early days, the colonies imported the British poor laws. These laws made a distinction between those who were unable to work due to their age, and/or physical health and those who were able-bodied but unemployed. The former group was assisted with cash or alternative forms of help from the government. The latter group was given public service employment in workhouses.

Throughout the 1800s welfare continued with attempts to reform how the government dealt with the poor. Some changes were made to help the poor move to work rather than continuing to need assistance. Social caseworkers visited the poor to attempt to train them in morals and create a work-ethic in them. I say let's bring this action back. If the founding fathers thought this was a good idea and it worked for them, then why can't we re-establish another program like this? Below I will outline the basic requirement for receiving welfare benefits. Now keep in mind the so-called entitlements were designed for the recipient to one-day work towards leaving the program on a definitive time table.

Basic Requirements for Welfare

- A basic lack of gainful employment opportunity through either lack of employment opportunity or lack of job skill.
- A commitment to self-sufficiency is necessary before any potential recipient can begin to receive benefits. Heads of households must enter into agreement that they will become self-sufficient within a certain time frame.
- A commitment of cooperation must be signed by heads of households that they will comply with and continue all rules and requirements while receiving aid.
- Dependent children must be living in the household. There are some exceptions, but generally all dependents must be within the home.
- All minors must be attending school during school days.
- All minors and dependents must be fully and appropriately immunized.

- You must be a legal and permanent resident of the state to which you are applying.
- You must be a citizen of the United States or a qualified non-citizen legal resident.
- All monetary resources must be divulged. This includes cash within the home, in checking/savings accounts and items of value in possession such as jewelry or electronics.
- A household financial budget must be created and adhered to.
- The recipient must be 18 years of age.

Here's a thought, why can't we add a requirement that recipients swear or attest to remain drug and/or alcohol dependent free (or enter a program) during the period of receiving benefits. Sorry, I was just thinking out loud, but back to what I was saying. These programs/entitlements include: Medicare and Medicaid, food stamps, supplemental security income, Housing Urban Development (HUD), temporary assistance for needy families (TANF), Head start, work study, and the granddaddy of them all Social Security. One in six Americans are receiving help from the government, just as fiscal austerity threatens to reduce some of this aid. The Great Recession has driven millions of people to the dole. Enrollment in Medicaid and food stamps are at record highs, while unemployment benefits remain at elevated levels. Many people depend on more than one program. I can attest that some people really need these programs to live but, there are way too many people out there that don't. Remember a government that provides for everything can also take away everything.

I will emphasize again that the goal of these programs/entitlements is to help individuals and families break the cycle of dependency on welfare. While some individuals rely too heavily on the welfare system, there are a great many more that simply need temporary assistance and use the welfare system as it was designed. Ben Franklin said that these welfare programs were designed to help the needy get back on their feet. They were not designed to make them feel comfortable about their situation, rather a little uncomfortable to urge them to recover as quickly as possible.

If you are one of those few individuals that believe social security alone will be enough to provide you with a comfortable retirement at a reasonable age, good luck. This program/entitlement has been around since 1937 and in 1940 about 220,000 people received monthly checks. By 2005, the number reached approximately 48 million, plus another 8 million received cash payments under supplemental security income. Social Security is expected to cover around 84 million people by 2030 and consume 6% of the nation's economy.

The program is only guaranteed to 2037 for full benefits, if there are no major changes in the program it should be able to pay 75% of benefits through 2083. There has been talk circulating about raising the retirement age to seventy years old, increasing social security payroll taxes and reducing initial payments. I can recall in 2010 when France raised their retirement age from fifty eight to sixty and the people were rioting in the streets, can you imagine what might happen here? All I'm saying is prepare yourself for it and make the necessary adjustments now while there is still time. I would much rather take the money that I have to pay towards social security each month and invest it on my own, but since I don't have a choice in the matter I will put my request in to receive my benefits as early as I can.

In 1965 President Lyndon Johnson used the umbrella of the Social Security Act to establish two new massive entitlement programs - -Medicare and Medicaid. Johnson explained that through this new law....every citizen will be able in his/her productive years to insure they will have coverage in their old age. This insurance will help pay for care in hospitals, in nursing homes, or in the home. And under a separate plan, help meet the fees of doctors.

Today Medicare covers most people age sixty-five and older; some people under sixty-five with disabilities. It covers most impatient hospital care, outpatient physical and speech therapy, ambulance services, some medical services, and most prescription drugs. Because Medicare pays providers directly, Medicare users have little incentive to behave cost-efficiently. Just like Social Security virtually everyone contributes to the system through a payroll tax, regardless of income level. Nineteen million people initially enrolled in Medicare and as of 2007 it covered approximately 44 million people. In 2030, Medicare is expected to cover 79 million people and consume 11% of the nation's economy.

Medicare along with Social Security is running up some serious IOU's that will punish our children and grandchildren for years to come. Unless Congress does something about it and the longer action is delayed, the greater the required adjustments will be, the larger the burden on future generations will be, and the more severe the detrimental economic impact will be on our nation. The Congressional Budget Office (CBO) projected that if Social Security, Medicare, and Medicaid go unchanged, by 2082 tax rate for the lowest tax bracket would increase from 10% to 25%; the tax rate on incomes in the current 25% bracket would have to be increased to 63%; and the tax rate for the highest bracket would have to be raised to from 35% to 88%.

Don't they realize that most of us hard-working Americans do not want to pay into this ponzi-scheme, especially if many of us don't believe it will be around when it is our time to collect? Here is a thought, why doesn't the federal government continue to pay our citizens who are currently getting social security until they are no longer here on this earth. The rest of us should have the option to stop paying into it and get a tax rebate until all the money we have paid into the system has been refunded back to us in tax cuts. Furthermore our younger generation should not have to pay into it at all. The CBO also warns that these programs are unsustainable and demand urgent attention. The Census Bureau reported that there are 46.6 million (another inflated number) people without health insurance.

Let's talk about President Obama's Health care reform. In 2008 ex-Democratic Speaker of the House Nancy Pelosi issued a statement declaring that 47 million American citizens are without health care. About 9.5 million were not United States citizens, another 17 million lived in households with incomes exceeding fifty thousand dollars a year and could purchase their own health care coverage if they chose to do so. 18 million of the 46.6 million uninsured were between the ages of eighteen and thirty-four, most of whom were in good health and not necessarily in the need for health-care coverage and most likely chose not to purchase it. So the 47 million uninsured figure used by Pelosi and others was widely inaccurate.

I was stationed in England for three years and saw first-hand how disastrous their government run health care system was. The waiting time for emergency care was horrendous. The waiting time for surgeries was a disaster. Patients wait between one and two years to receive hip or knee replacement surgeries. Children must travel to the United States to receive certain cancer treatments that are unavailable under the British health system. In a recent survey conducted in England as many as one in three family and hospital doctors believes that elderly patients should not be given free treatment if it is unlikely to help them over the long term. They believe smokers should be denied bypass surgery and that obese people should not be eligible for the hip and knee replacement surgeries. So if it is not working there, why would anyone believe it will be successful here?

<u>The National Debt (Nightmare)</u>

The United States has had public debt since its inception (235 years ago). Debts incurred during the American Revolutionary War and under the Articles of Confederation led to the first yearly reported value $75,463,476.52 on January 01, 1791. From 1796 to 1811 there were 14 surpluses and only 2 deficits. The second dramatic growth spurt of the debt occurred because of the Civil War. The debt was just $65 million in 1860, but passed $1 billion in 1863 and had reached $2.7 billion following the war. The next period of major growth in debt came during WWI reaching $25.5 billion. It was followed by 11 straight years of surpluses that saw the debt reduced by 36%.

The debt went from $16 billion to $260 billion from 1930 – 1950 mostly because the Great Depression and WWII. After this period the debt tripled in size from $260 billion in 1950 to $909 billion in 1980. During the Bush administration, the debt increased from $5.7 trillion in January 2001 to $10.7 trillion in December 2008 (8years). Currently under President Obama's administration, the debt has increased at record levels from $10.7 trillion to $14.3 trillion by April 2011 (2 years). At this pace the Obama administration will have spent and/ or created more debt than all the other presidencies combined in just 4 years. These levels are unsustainable and if something isn't done soon we may reach a point of no return.

How long has it been since our country has seen a surplus? That question is really debatable and I have seen several sets of numbers. The Clinton administration claimed to have had a surplus in 2000, but the numbers do not reflect that to be true. The last real surplus this country has seen was in 1957 under the Eisenhower administration. I'm sure we can all agree that has been too long ago. Forty-percent of our debt is owed to ourselves (Federal Reserve, the central bank of the United States, and to other government accounts). The remaining 60% of the debt is privately held by individuals, corporations, states, and foreign governments to include Japan, China, and the United Kingdom being the biggest holders of our debt.

The Debt Ceiling

The debt ceiling is simply a cap on how much money the United States Federal government can owe. If the debt ceiling is reached then the U.S. would be forbidden from incurring any more debt. The debt ceiling has been raised 74 times since 1962 and 10 times since 2001. Guess what….Our debt ceiling has been reached again. Our current debt ceiling is $14.3 trillion and our current debt is at 14.33, so the hot debate amongst our fearless leaders is the raising of the debt ceiling again or letting the government shut down, either way we are screwed. If you really want to see some depressing numbers go to http://www.usdebtclock.org/ the

44

numbers move faster than a fan. The other interesting numbers are that out of the 311 million people that live in this country give or take 50 – 100 million or so due to all the illegal's in this country that go uncounted, there is only 111 million taxpayers. Each taxpayer is in debt $128,681, that is depressing I thought I was doing a good enough job incurring debt on my own without the help from the government.

Immigration Part I

Immigration to the United States has been a major source of population growth and cultural changes throughout most of our history. As of 2008, the United States accepts more legal immigrants as permanent residents than all other countries in the world combined. 1,046,539 persons were naturalized as United States citizens in 2008. The leading emigrating countries to the United States were Mexico, India, Philippines and more recently the Middle East. Family reunification accounts for approximately two-thirds of legal immigration to the United States every year. The problem has been once they get here they are populating very rapidly. By 2050 the Hispanic population will have tripled to 102 million, or about 24 percent of the nation. Meanwhile the white population grew by 2.5 percent, the black population by 5.3 percent, the Asian population by 21.5 percent, and the Hispanic population grew by almost 28 percent in 2005. As a matter of fact Hispanics just took over as the number one minority group in America in 2011.

Unlike the immigrants of Ellis Island in the beginning, it appears that the new immigrants do not want anything to do with becoming Americans. Ellis Island was the gateway for millions of immigrants to the United States as the site of the nation's busiest immigration station from 1892 – 1954. According to the US Bureau of Immigration over 12 million immigrants were processed there. Today over 100 million Americans – one third of the population can trace their ancestry to the immigrants who first arrived in America at Ellis Island.

Those immigrants came to America for a chance at a better life and gave their lives to become dedicated patriotic Americans. We have to stop the madness of letting illegal immigrants come into our borders at will. The southwest part of our country is being invaded. The simple solution would be to enforce the laws that we currently have in place. If you read Article IV, section 4 of the Constitution it states that the United States shall guarantee to every State in this Union a Republican Form of Government, and shall protect each of them against Invasion; and on Application of the Legislature, or of the Executive against domestic violence.

The reason why this section is included in this chapter is because of the stress that these numbers are putting on not just the Border States, but the country. For example native-born Californians have begun to depart. The California they grew up in and loved has morphed into "Mexifornia." Fed up with rising crime rates and rising taxes to subsidize illegal aliens about 100 whites leave California each year, California is becoming a third-world state. They are not alone, and if we do not do something soon, it will be too late.

We are being invaded, why hasn't the National Guard been activated and protecting our borders? Historians estimate that less than one million immigrants crossed the Atlantic during the 17th and 18th centuries. The 1790 act limited naturalization to "free white persons", it expanded it to include blacks in 1860 and Asians in the 1950s. Nearly eight million immigrants came to the United States from 2000 – 2005, more than any other five year period in the nation's history. Almost half entered illegally. 1.1 million Immigrants were granted legal residence in 2009. Immigrants posted a net gain of 656,000 jobs since June 2009.

"There are fifteen million unemployed workers in America and eight million illegal immigrants in the labor force. We could cut unemployment in half simply by reclaiming the jobs taken by illegal workers", says Republican Lamar Smith (R-Texas). Recent polls in the United States by Zogby/New Global Initiatives also show an unprecedented 1.5 million Americans have already decided to leave the United States and another 1.8 million, calling themselves likely to leave. Ronald Reagan once said, "A country that can't control its borders isn't really a country anymore. " We need to start adhering to those words now, before it is too late.

Welcome to the Disappearance of Las Vegas

The once booming Las Vegas region has led the United States in home foreclosures for forty five straight months and a whopping 80% of houses are "underwater" at the writing of this book. Meaning that they now owe more than their home is worth. The entire town is basically foreclosed on. Gangs are setting up shop and the town looks vacant. Las Vegas was once the prime example of the American boom town. This city has enjoyed continuous growth in visitors and population since the 1950s. Its population jumped to nearly 2.6 million residents. There was no place in America where real-estate ran so rampant and prices surged so quickly, but what goes up must come down. Since the "Great Recession" Las Vegas' economy has started to plummet. Nevada leads America in unemployment at 14.7% and the worse housing market in the country.

The Motor City isn't far behind. Detroit's population shrank by more than 25% in the last decade, according to Census statistics reported in the New York Times. The city's population fell to 713,777 in 2010, a drop of almost 240,000 residents. Detroit is not the only place dealing with an oversupply of housing. The Census also shows that 18% of Florida homes—more than 1.6 million properties are vacant. With more than four million foreclosures in just over a year and rising gas prices, more and more cities will look like ghost towns in coming years. We are in for a bumpy ride, strap-in, get prepared, and pray.

As long as we are talking about disappearing we might as well mention the middle class. Middle class is defined as those aged 30 to 69 with forty to one hundred thousand dollars in household income or twenty five to one hundred thousand dollars in investable assets and those aged 25 to 29 with income investable assets of twenty five to one hundred thousand dollars. Since "The Great Recession" the middle class started empting out their savings accounts due to the massive layoffs/job losses, home foreclosures, and rising cost of health care and utilities.

The middle class think they need three hundred thousand dollars to fund their retirement, but on average have only saved twenty thousand dollars according to a recent survey conducted by Wells Fargo & Co. The average American has saved less than seven percent of their income for their retirement nest egg, and will likely have to keep working in retirement to supplement their income. Seventy percent of survey respondents aged 50 to 59 believe Social Security will be needed to contribute to their retirement income. Now entering 2011 and savings gone, retirement accounts/401ks are the next to go. Soon there will be nothing left to takeout and then what? This is what remains to be seen. If the economy doesn't improve soon, third world status is right around the corner, and the disappearance of the middle class is just the beginning.

The Selling of Citizenship has just been Discounted

More signs of the collapsing of our economy is the selling of citizenship. The EB-5 program is the green card/citizenship program. Ten thousand visas are set aside each year to encourage foreign investors to come into the country and create jobs by starting new businesses. If they agreed to invest one million dollars, foreigners can get a visa, apply for green cards, and become permanent residents if after two years they've made good on their promise to invest, create ten jobs (cannot be family members). After five years with a green card the holder can apply for citizenship. Unfortunately the EB-5 program has never come close to maxing out.

According to the United States Citizenship and Immigration Services, just 1,028 people applied for EB-5 status and 996 were approved. The fact of the matter is that United States citizenship is just not that appealing anymore, especially when we have millions of illegal immigrants pouring in to our country every year and not having to go through the citizenship programs and immediately reaping the benefits of our welfare system. More and more states are starting to go bankrupt.

The really disturbing part is that foreign governments of some of these illegal immigrants are helping them get here through unethical official government action. So our leadership decided to lower the price of admission to five hundred thousand dollars instead of the one million to try and entice more foreigners to take advantage of the newly revised EB-5 program. Meanwhile we have about one hundred and fifty thousand Americans voluntarily retiring to other countries per year, looking for a better place to live and make their money go further and that number has been increasing every year over the last five.

Towns Where Land is Free

Just to put the finishing touches on how bad the economy is there are still some towns in the United States where land is free. That's right, free. As small towns are suffering from the extended down economy people are fleeing the rural areas towards more urban living for better chances of finding jobs. So if you are well-to-do and tired of the rat race, traffic, constant lines, and love the outdoors this deal might be right up your alley. Unfortunately I'm not in a position to take advantage of a deal like this, but here is the list:

Marne, Iowa population of 149 and about 60 miles from Omaha
New Richland, Minnesota population 1,200 and about 75 miles from the twin cities.
Kansas – several locations
Beatrice, Nebraska   population 12,564 and about 40 miles from Lincoln.

Muskegon, Michigan population 174,344, looking for small business opportunities to help create jobs. Twenty five jobs gets you five acres, seventy five jobs gets you twenty acres, and one hundred jobs gets you over twenty acres.

Curtis, Nebraska   population 832

Camden, Maine   population 4,052 is offering free land to small businesses that will help create at least 24 new jobs.

These deals are not for the faint of heart. If you are prepared to leave the rat race and build your dream house from ground up, then check these deals out.

History of the Tax Code

The first instance of a federal income tax was adopted by Congress in 1861 to help pay for the Civil War. The 1862 law levied a 3% tax on incomes above eight hundred dollars, rising to 5% for incomes above ten thousand dollars. Rates were raised in 1864, this income tax was repealed in 1872, but a new income tax was enacted as part of the Wilson-Gorman Tariff Act in 1894.

In 1909 Congress proposed the Sixteenth Amendment, which became part of the Constitution in 1913 when it was ratified by the required number of States. Congress re-adopted the income tax that same year, levying a 1% tax on net personal incomes above three thousand dollars with six percent surtax on incomes above five hundred thousand dollars. By 1918, the top rate of the income tax was increased to 77% (on incomes over 1 million dollars) to finance World War I.

The top marginal rate was reduced to 58% in 1922, to 25% in 1925, and finally to 24% in 1929. In 1932 the top marginal tax rate was increased to 63% during the Great Depression and steadily increased. In 2001, President George W. Bush proposed and Congress accepted an eventual lowering of the top marginal rate to 35%. However, this was to be done in stages: The measure had a sunset provision and was scheduled to expire in Jan 2011. The Bush tax cuts were extended by President Obama and Congress for at least two more years. When the rates would return to those adopted by President Clinton at 39.6%, unless an agreement can be met to change the law before then.

When asked how to fix the national deficit people will always say tax the rich more. Let's take a look at this statistic. The top 10% earners in this country pay 90% of the taxes. The bottom 50% only pay 2% of the taxes in this country. What is happening here is that millions of Americans are not paying any taxes. So believe me when I tell you that is not the answer. The only reasonable answer is less spending by our government, not higher taxes for the rich.

One unique aspect of the federal income tax in the United States is that the government uses citizenship in addition to residency in determining whether a person's income is subject to taxation. All U.S. citizens, including those who do not reside in the United States are subject to income tax on their worldwide income. This brings in new concerns and debates over illegal immigration. How many illegals are in the labor force today and not paying any federal income taxes?

While taxes have been certain, they have been far from being consistent, ironically it was taxes that led Americans to revolt against the British in 1773. Colonists objected a tea tax, boarded three ships and destroyed the tea by throwing it into the Boston Harbor. Protestors had successfully prevented the unloading of taxed tea in three colonies. This movement was called the Boston Tea Party and a key event in the growth of the American Revolution, which began near Boston in 1775. America was basically tax-free for much of its early history.

The Federal Tax Code started out as a simple document but has turned out to be a monstrosity of several thousand pages about ten times longer than the Bible that no one can fully understand. Has the tax code become too complex to be Constitutional? By the time you read it the rules would be obsolete. There have been more than 4,400 changes to the tax code over the past decade, or more than one change a day. Why don't the courts force a tax simplification? Below is a list of some of the taxes we as American citizens are forced to pay:

Accounts Receivable	Accumulated Earnings Tax
Valorem Tax	Alternative Min. Tax
Aviation Fuel Tax	Capital Gains Tax
Cement License Tax	Cigarette Tax
Coal Severance Tax	Coal Gross Proceeds Tax
Consumer Counsel Tax	Consumption Tax
Corporate Income Tax	Corporation Income Tax
Court Fines	Custom Duty
Death Tax	Dog License Tax
Electrical Energy Tax	Estate/Inheritance Tax
Federal Income Tax	Federal Unemployment
Fishing License Tax	Food Service Tax
Fuel Permit Tax	Gas Guzzler Tax
Gasoline Tax	Generation Transfer Tax
Gift Tax	Gross Production
Hospital Utilization Tax	Hunting License Tax
Inventory Tax	IRS Interest Charges
IRS Penalties Tax	Kiddie Tax
Land Value Tax	Liquor License Tax
Local Tax	Lodging Facility Tax
Luxury Tax	Marriage License Tax
Medicare Tax	Metal Mines Gross Tax
Nursing Facilities Bed Tax	Oil & Natural Gas Tax
Parking Meter Tax	Payroll Tax
Professional Privilege	Property Tax
Public Contractor's Tax	Public Service Tax
Public Utility Tax	Real Estate Tax
Real Estate Transfer Tax	Resort Tax
Rental Vehicle Sales Tax	Sales Tax
Self-Employment Tax	School Tax
Septic Permit Tax	Social Security Tax
State Income Tax	State Unemployment Tax
State-wide 911 Fee tax	Surtax Tax
Tariffs	Telephone Excise Tax
Tobacco Products Tax	Toll Road Tax

Toll Bridge Tax	Toll Tunnel Tax
Tonnage Tax	Traffic Fines Tax
Trailer Fee Tax	Use Tax
Utility Tax	Vehicle Reg. Tax
Vehicle Sales Tax	Watercraft Reg. Tax
Well Permit Tax	Workers Comp. Tax

Wholesale Energy Trans. Tax …..And last but not least the famous Double Tax…Now that was one hell of a lineup. And remember our ancestor's before us were pissed off about a tea tax and went to war…….

In recent years the scope of federal control over society has widened as politicians of both parties have favored nationalizing many state, local, and private activities. New York may lose ground as an international financial center, falling behind London, which shares Manhattan's language but not its less popular nationality, currency, and financial products. Over the next two decades, the biggest gainers are foreseen to be Asian, but great expectations are divided among Singapore, Hong Kong, Tokyo, and Shanghai.

However, should the United States decide to imitate the commitments of high-value added manufacturers and exporters like Germany, Japan, and Switzerland, some success would be likely, especially given the weakness of the dollar. Woodrow Wilson said, "The ideal government was for every man to be left alone and not interfered with, except when he interfered with somebody else; and that the best government was the government that did as little governing as possible." I agree with you Mr. Wilson, but will we ever be fortunate enough to see it come true?

Blogs in relation to this Chapter (We the People have Spoken)

- *If we do not attempt to reduce our national deficit, instead of having 50 million unfortunate Americans living in poverty, we will have 250 million. Luckily the unfortunates are too lazy to get off the couch and work - - much less vote.*

- *On retiring early – So you stay in a small dark house and never go out and have any fun until you reach your goal. Then you retire with no friends and bad knees. I'd rather try and enjoy life while I save and retire at sixty with bad knees.*

- *The Great Recession as it has become known is most certainly NOT over. In fact, it's gotten worse.*

- *The Gen-Xer's wanted it all, designer jeans, fancy cars, every electric gadget imaginable and the big expensive house to match their egos. They had everything but common sense. To be wise, to save, and to live within your means is too much sacrifice. You're enjoying your retirement now.*

- *Forget the numbers—our economy is in the crapper and people are struggling to keep a roof over their heads and food on the table. There is one major factor that I have never seen addressed. Many people who have managed to find some sort of employment are working outside their fields, surviving on part-time jobs and earning far less than they did previously. I know—I'm one of them. I could get health insurance through my job—if I could afford it on my $9/hr. part-time job. I have to rely on public health clinics and eat ramin noodles and pray that my ancient car miraculously keeps running. I guess death is the new retirement.*

- *To those who are telling us to "swallow our pride" and get a job, any job even if it's at Wal-Mart, etc. First off, the notion that we are somehow too proud to take a job at Wal-Mart is wrong and somewhat offensive. Try feeding a family of four, as well as paying your mortgage, bills, and car payment on minimum wage, it's impossible. If you have done it, then congratulations you are one of the lucky ones. In most cases you get more money staying on unemployment. This has nothing to do with pride; it has everything to do with survival.*

- *The government needs to encourage its citizens to be creative in making money in a downed economy - - not give more handouts. Half of us are tired of working so the other half never lifts a hand, and are encouraged by government bailouts, handouts, entitlements, etc., If you're in a hole, then stop digging.*

- *I hope soon that folks taking advantage of the welfare system (90% of the liberal left) cannot afford to put food on their tables and are forced to emigrate to Mexico and/or Canada….That would be a great day in America…if you can't pay your fair share, then get out of the country! Live on someone else's dime…not mine!*

- *They had "99 weeks" of welfare and that is enough. We (the taxpayers) need to be able to have a little left in our paychecks after all the re-distribution of wealth is finished stealing too much of our money. Lower all forms of welfare and reduce the re-distribution of our wealth today and forever. When do the unemployment benefits become the un-willing to work benefits?*

- *These stock market numbers have been thrown out there for years and historically speaking they are true. But we live in a totally different economy now, especially if you put all your eggs in one basket and you get stuck in a down decade right before you retire. Diversify!!!!*

- *If the job numbers get much worse, I could wind up sleeping instead of sitting on this bench.*

- *The recession is over? Wow, I didn't know. Now just maybe I can find a bigger box to live in.*
- *Who cares about the economy when the government pumps up the stock market with tax payer dollars? I'll just sit back, collect unemployment and food stamps while watching my million dollar portfolio grow. Only in America!!*

- *News Flash!!!! Jobless claims rise, as people find it more productive to sit at home and surf the internet rather than find a job or learn a new trade. These are the same people who will complain about someone on welfare, but whine when their unemployment benefits run out. Oh Wait! But you say you paid into the system? Buddy, we all pay into the system and the system was not meant for you to keep getting welfare (oops, I mean unemployment) extensions forever. Eventually you're going to have to get back to work. Don't be afraid. You can do it. Just like your parents and grandparents before you have done.*

- *All this unemployment and I can't hire 3 tractor drivers. The people don't want to sweat.*

- *My neighbor, a laid off teacher, is hoping that she doesn't get called back to work because her extended unemployment and the lack of need for child care is financial incentive enough to stay home....this may be the new norm.*

- *Get on welfare and work under the table, that's what's going on, fraud everywhere you look, that's why most of us honest people will have to work till we die!!*

III

Preparing for the worse

"Most people don't plan to fail, they fail to plan"
-John L. Beckley
"Democracy is two wolves and a lamb deciding on what's for dinner.
Liberty is a well-armed lamb"
-Ben Franklin

In this chapter I will attempt to educate you on how to prepare for the worse. It is never too early to start preparing; the first step should be socking away as much money as you can (in case banks start failing again). Most of the financial information can be found in chapter four. It is good practice to have tangible items on hand for trading when and if money becomes worthless. I know it is hard to fathom and it may sound extreme, but is it really?

It doesn't take a rocket scientist to see that the events of the last several years may become the norm. Is it really that farfetched to imagine that if the state of this nation gets any worse we may revert back to the dark ages or become a third world country? Things may not get any better, we can just pray they don't get much worse. But if you are awake to what is going on around you and make plans for the worse to happen, you will not be floored or caught with your pants down when and if it does.

You know it's sad when the hard working, providing for his/her family, tax paying, trying to do the right thing American Christian has become the minority in this country. The majority of folks want to be taken care of by the government. They want more stimulus, welfare, unemployment benefits, and as many so-called entitlements as they can get for nothing. The government doles out more than thirty-five percent of the nation's budget in welfare benefits at the writing of this book and that is up from twenty-one percent in 2000. I know I have said this more than once but I want it to sink in, a government that provides for everything can also take everything.

These entitlement babies don't want to work and they have given up on providing for their families. So if the majority gets off their butts and votes for the candidates that will give them those entitlements (like the ones we have running the country now), then the rest of us are pretty much screwed. If you don't believe me take a look at these numbers. According to the most recent census data, 222 million Americans were eligible to vote and 93 million paid no income taxes. There was a time in history when only land owners could vote, why not implement a new policy stating that only taxpayers (real taxpayers) can vote. We all know it is not happening that way. An additional 24 million taxpayers will pay a minimal amount of income taxes – less than 5% of their income and less than $1,000 annually. So the hardworking minority will have to go to great lengths to make a difference. The great American patriot Samuel Adams said, "It does not require a majority to prevail, but rather an irate, tireless minority, keen to set brush fires in people's minds." Get motivated, get educated, and get prepared before it is too late.

Zombie Apocalypse?

Our culture is full of tales of the undead walking the earth. But is a zombie apocalypse really possible? Why not and here's why: Parasites that turn victims into mindless zombie like slaves are fairly common. Toxoplasmosis Gondi is a bug that infects rats, but can only breed in the intestines of a cat. The parasite knows it needs to get inside the cat to live. So the rat is being programmed to get eaten by the cat, and doesn't even know it. By the way a good portion of the population on earth is infected with toxoplasmosis and don't know it. Studies show that the infected see a change in their personality and have a high chance of going insane. Imagine if half the world suddenly had no instinct for self-preservation or rational thought. It sounds far-fetched doesn't it? Or does it?

United States government researchers reported that more than 45 million American, or twenty percent of the United States had some form of mental illness last year, and 11 million had a serious illness. Young adults' ages 18 – 25 had the highest level of mental illness at thirty percent, with those aged fifty and older at the lowest with 13.7%. Can these not be forms of zombies? To add insult to injury we have 40 million more zombies that drive around drunk (30 million) and or drugged (10 million) each year. My definition of a zombie is one of the millions of desperate people out of work, lost their homes, has no family and that has given up and will do whatever it takes to survive. Some of these people will be jiggling your door knobs during the day or night while the rest of us are at work or asleep.

Their intentions are to take what you have worked for and earned and make it their own. That could be the new zombie apocalypse if things don't get better in a hurry. I'm a certified zombie hunter, are you? That leads me into my next topic; Home Invasions. If you're not home it's a robbery if you are home it's a home invasion. Are you ready for what might happen to you and your family if you are caught in this situation? Can you defend yourself and your family if this unfortunate situation happens to you as it does to 1 in every 4 homes since the "Great Recession"? Then please read on.........

Home Invasion Part I

I always told myself not to worry about things you can't control. Home invasions and robberies are one of those things, but you can be prepared and try to deter these events from happening to you. So I want to introduce the four D's. Deter, Detect, Delay and Defend! Let's start with the first one Deter; lighting. After all a bad guy doesn't want the local cop on patrol or any one for that matter to see him sneaking around your house or loading your stuff into his truck.

Alarms and the signs that go with them are great deterrents. But be mindful that even after the alarm goes off you may have ten to fifteen minutes before a police officer arrives on the scene. Can you fight three armed robbers for that long? Along the lines of deter and detect a man's best friend can really play a big part of both. A good dog (or two) can go a long way in deterring bad guys and warning you when they approach. The delay phase can best be summed up as "hardening the target". Remember, home invaders don't care if you are there to witness their actions. If they are determined to come in, make them work for it. Keep your doors and windows locked even when you are home. Don't unlock and open the door for a stranger unless you are prepared to deal with them. This isn't 1955, even kids as old as nine or ten years old have cell phones. The old "I need to borrow your phone" excuse should not work anymore. If they truly have a roadside emergency, tell them politely that you will call the police for them. If an intruder decides to force their way in, they should not be able to do it quietly. A thirty second delay is long enough when it comes to reaction time, of course longer is better.

Determine just how tough it is to get into your house. Randomly walk around and check for soft spots. The last resort, after all other means have failed is to use violent force. The felons that are trying to smash your door in are not going to be timid. In the real world your attackers are going to be younger, stronger and usually have a few friends with them. The best defense against this attack is violent force applied with a firearm. If all you have is a small handgun on you at the time of the attack, use it until you can get to your long gun. As I have told all my friends nothing says "Get out of my Home" like the racking of a 12 gauge shotgun. Keep in mind that you may have to use deadly force. If you feel like you can't pull the trigger on a murderer or a rapist then don't have a gun in your home. For those of us that choose to have several guns in their home, get to the range and continue to practice. Every responsible adult and teenage child should know how to use a gun. In the middle of an attack is not the time to figure out how the safety works or how to load a gun, by then it is too late.

A grab and go bag is what you will need in a worst-case emergency if you have to evacuate your home. Keep it safe in your house packed with as many essentials as you can think of, but keep it small enough to be able to just run out the door with. Normally these bags will consist of a pistol, ammo, cell phone, survival knife, meals ready to eat (MRE), emergency blanket, pack of bic lighters(this is not the time to be cute and light a fire with two sticks), chlorine tablets, small solar powered radio, batteries and maybe a sling shot with some ball bearings. Most of these items exist in my grab and go bag with some other items I did not mention, but I'm sure you get the point by now. Take at least an annual inventory of the items in the bag and add items as you see fit.

Last but not least I advise you to start loading up on can goods, bottled water, and other non-perishable items. I was listening to the Glenn Beck show on Sirius Patriot radio, when I heard a testimony of a young family with six children who survived 17 months of unemployment by the husband and wife. They accomplished this amazing feat by preparing for this situation when they both were working. They started stock piling food and saving all they could before tragedy struck their family. They gave God his glory, made it through with lots of prayers, never giving up, and never taking one red cent of welfare/entitlement benefits from the government. This is the perfect example of preparing for the worst and praying for the best.

Self Defense for the Soul (Home Invasion Part II)

In today's uncertain economy, the unemployed are not the only people stressed out about work. Even those of us with jobs are worried. You can be fired, laid off at any time for no reason. You see and read about it every day. We are experiencing an era with record job losses, record home foreclosures, and it has happened to family, friends and co-workers we know and whom some have nowhere to go. The scary thing is that most of us are only a crisis away from being in the same boat.

These unemployed and near-penniless individuals can easily switch to a life of crime, as things get worse civil disorder can erupt in cities and towns nationwide. The motivation to acquire and keep firearms is there for two reasons; protect against unrest of hard times, and the concern that the current presidency will mean radical measures in banning or restricting the sale and ownership of guns. Law enforcement officers across the country are also being laid off in droves and retiring cops are not being replaced because the state of the economy has devastated public service funding. It is getting so bad that sheriff's, local cops, and judges are telling people that they have to start protecting themselves. That is why the crown jewel of the Bill of Rights also known as the second amendment which gives us the right to keep and bear arms is so important to each and every one of us. But employing this right takes common sense, self-discipline, and knowledge. It also requires the physical and mechanical abilities to stop those who would murder or cripple.

Fears of home invasions and increased gang/drug violence have sparked gun sales and conceal carry permits to an all-time high. The Department of Justice show five to eight thousand home invasions are reported every day. Thirty eight percent of assaults and sixty percent of rapes occur during home invasions. One in every four homes will experience a break-in or home invasion.

During the "Great Recession" home invasions were through the roof. While most people fear that their home will be burglarized when they are away cannot fathom the fear they will feel when becoming victims of a home invasion. Keep in mind that most robberies occur between 9a.m. – 5 p.m. when most people are at work, while most home invasions occur between 6 p.m. – 6 a.m. Home invaders want someone to be home so they can get access to more valuables such as bank accounts and combinations for safes. Two, three, and sometime four or more criminals will break into a home whether it is occupied or not to rob, terrorize, rape, and sometimes kill the families inside. Home invaders are vicious and violent characters that have and will continue to commit horrible atrocities against families. Below is a checklist that you need to burn to memory to help you prevent and act if you become a victim. The statistics show that a lot of us will be:

Preventing Home Invasions

1. If you have an alarm system, make sure your signs/stickers are posted. Even if you don't get some signs/stickers anyway.
2. Use motion lights around your house.
3. Make sure that your locks not only are solid but look solid from the outside.
4. Keep valuables placed where they are not visible from open windows.
5. Practice trash discipline. If you purchased a big ticket item, cut up the packaging and remove shipping labels.
6. Get an outside dog or two to help deter and warn you if an intruder is near.
7. Use peep holes and use caution when opening the doors for strangers.
8. Keep doors and windows lock even when you are home. Make sure your windows have the safety hinges installed so windows cannot open all the way.
9. Do frequent checks for soft spots in entering your house.

During Home Invasion

1. Know your surroundings; identify household objects in every room that you can use as improvised weapons.
2. Act as quickly as possible. The more time your attacker has to restrain/control you, the less likely you'll be able to cause a safe outcome for you and your family.
3. As a foundation, you have got your body to use as a weapon. Learn the best parts of your body to use as weapons (elbows, knees) and best places to attack your attacker. If you have firearms or other weapons place them close to where you may need them.
4. If an attacker successfully bluffs their way into your home you may find yourself at the mercy of weapons. In this case comply with their requests in order to prevent physical violence or bodily harm. If you are victimized give the police an accurate description of the attackers and anything else that might be useful.

Seven signs of the Apocalypse

Being a man of Christian faith I have heard about and I am very aware of the seven signs of the apocalypse. No matter what your religion it is hard for anyone to be oblivious to the things going on in the world. Things such as war, famine, natural disasters, and all the hate around us are definitely signs that some parts of the world are not good places to be. Mathew 24 speaks of wars on a global scale, famine, pestilence (sickness & disease), lawlessness (crime), people having no love for one another, and earthquakes.

Timothy 3,:1-5, speak of actions of people in the last days; men will be lovers of themselves, lovers of money, self-assuming, haughty, blasphemers, disobedient to parents, unthankful, disloyal, having no natural affection, lovers of pleasures rather than lovers of God. Jesus says in Mathew 24:14 that these signs are good news, because his kingdom is coming closer. For those of us that are of the Christian faith, we cannot forget about the seven signs of the apocalypse that the bible has taught us.

Being a man of faith, I have read the Bible in its entirety at least four times, and each time I read it I find more interesting events that happen to pertain to my life and the time I'm going through them. It's simply amazing. The book of Revelations is not a comfortable read and it was not meant to be. The seven signs are not called signs but seals or vials. Each seal is not very specific either, but if you read them for yourselves I'm sure your interpretation will be close to what I have listed below. Although the opening of each seal in turn has a spectacular result, the seventh seal is far greater because it is divided into seven trumpets, and its seventh trumpet is further divided into seven bowls (vials). And reading through it you will find that the events being talked about and described have already happened or are happening now. You be the judge:

1. Religious Conquest (White Horse)
2. Conflict and War (Red Horse)
3. Famine and Drought (Black Horse)
4. Death (Pale Horse)
5. Vision of Martyrdom or Martyrs
6. Cosmic Disturbances (earthquakes/sun blackens out) or Heavenly Signs and the marking of the 144 thousand
7. Prelude to the 7 trumpets and Final Judgment

__Immigration Part II__

I touched on this subject earlier in chapter two, but I also think it deserves a little more attention due to the severity of the problem. Also if nothing is done about this issue, we need to start preparing ourselves on how to deal with it. As I also said before in this book, that I do not have a problem with immigration as long as it is legal and I also went into a little history of immigration in chapter two. As long as immigrants come in legally, with conviction, and loyalty to this great country, this would not be an issue. But unfortunately this is not what has been happening as of late.

Due to the recent state of our country, the 2112 subsidy programs (and counting), free education, housing subsidies, food stamps, welfare checks, supplemental security income, earned income tax credits, and the talk of Obama care, immigrants legal and illegal are pouring in by the thousands on a daily basis. Our founding fathers believed that before immigrants could become American citizens they must embrace our language, customs, and habits, as well as our principles.

The problem is that this is not happening. It seems as the opposite is happening, we see bi-lingual signs as we drive through our towns, we see other races trying to push their religion on us and conform to their culture. Not only is this not happening but masses of Mexican immigrants have been aided by their own government to get in through our borders undetected. They have prepared brochures on how to evade Border Patrol, where they can pick up documents, and how they can sign up for welfare. Mexico's National Human Rights Commission (HRC) was caught preparing seventy thousand maps for border crossers in 2006. They also distributed a 32-page manual, titled "The Guide for the Mexican Migrant", with tips on how to cross the border and evade detection. Why don't our boys do something to stop the madness? We are all standing by to hear the answer to that question.

According to the Immigration US Code Title 8, Section 1325; any alien who (1) enters or attempts to enter the United States at any time or place other than as designated by immigration officers, or (2) eludes examination or inspection by immigration officers. Shall, for the first commission of any such offense, be fined under title 18 or imprisoned not more than six months, or both, and, for a subsequent commission of any such offense, be fined under title 18, or imprisoned not more than two years, or both.

So once again we ask the question how approximately two thousand people can willfully ignore this statute daily, making illegal immigration a national crisis. No one knows for sure but estimates of our illegal population ranges from 15 to 35 million; and growing by the day. Americans are begging Congress, mayors, governors, or anyone who will listen to simply just enforce our laws. But it seems no one is listening.

The United States of Arabia?

Radical Islam has been referred to an "Islamofascism", and rightfully so. It is totalitarian and authoritarian. Its leaders advocate the overthrow of democratic governments and law because this ideology respects no government or rule of law except the rule of strict Islamic Shariah law. The rights and liberties of free people, as expressed in our documents such as the *Declaration of Independence* and the *Constitution of the United States*, will be completely eradicated if this ideology prevails.

September 11, 2001 at 0846 in the morning woke America up to just how real this threat really is. Radical Islamist demonstrated they were ready, willing and able to take on any city, culture, or country – even the most powerful nation in the world. Please do not be fooled into thinking that 911 was a fluke and could not happen again. This is what they want us to think.

The 911 attacks were committed by Muslim extremist in the name of holy war against the West. They used the Koran and Islamic principles to justify their actions. Their goal was to bring jihad to America, unleashing a clash of civilizations. Across the world Islamists seek to impose a world Muslim calaphite based on Shariah law.

After 911 Americans still perceive a mosque as a Muslim Church, refer to the Koran as the Islamic Bible, and equate sheikhs with priests and rabbis. Nothing could be further from the truth. Mosques are frequently used to preach hatred and killing in the name of Allah, and a place where militants can hide, store ammo, and discuss strategy of war. The Koran unlike the Bible calls for political movements for which Muslims must fight, kill, and subjugate those of other faiths until Islam rules the world. And sheikhs are political figures who urge their followers to fight and become martyrs in the name of Allah.

Since 911, there have been more than ten thousand Islamic terrorist attacks worldwide carried out by men and women who believe that dying for their religious beliefs is more important than life itself. Here is a red flag, a congressional report on homeland security by the committee on investigations acknowledged the threat of terrorist organizations sneaking into the United States through the Mexican border. These illegal's also known as other than Mexican (OTM) are crossing the Mexican border at alarming rates. These OTMs are nationals of Iran, Syria, Pakistan, Afghanistan, and Iraq. How long will it be before a nuclear or biological bomb is smuggled in through our almost unprotected borders?

Europe couldn't imagine what would happen to them when they opened up their borders to Muslims three generations ago. But today, third generation radicals are undertaking Western Europe with a militant, extremist agenda. And they are doing it with riots, rape, murder, beatings, burnings, and running native citizens out of their homes. But Europe was just a blueprint for the eventual cultural collision planned for America, and it's already arrived at a city near you. Make no mistake about it, terrorist cleverly disguise themselves behind the freedoms that you and I enjoy, and they are living among us. They have traded their swords for AK-47's, RPG's, TNT, and missiles. They are spreading their oil wealth around the world to bring Islam back. Their time of moderation and watered-down religion is over, and the Islam of Mohammed is back.

Brigette Gabriel, the author of *"They Must be Stopped"*, advises us to get organized, inform other interested people of what is happening, and join ACT (www.actforamerica.org). Act will provide news and commentary on matters related to national security, terrorism, and the spread of Islamofascism. They can connect you with others in your community, wherever you are, and provide you with educational material. Call your congressman or the White House with your concerns on these issues, every call is counted and considered (White House 202-456-1111). Keep your self informed, educated, and aware as well as others.

With numerous mosques and temples already here in America they want to build one near ground zero. Ground zero is where the war came home to America. And they have the gall to want to build a mosque in the area of the attacks. If we let this happen we have all but given in to radical Islam and you should be preparing yourself for all the horrors that will happen next…..

"Fight and kill the disbelievers wherever you find them, take them captive, harass them, lie in wait and ambush them using every stratagem of war." *(Koran 9:5)*

"Same ye slew, and ye made captive some. And he caused you to inherit their land and their houses and their wealth, and land ye have not trodden…" (Koran 33:26-27)

<u>Anchor Babies</u>

I know this is another touchy subject and I am by no means saying all illegal/legal immigrants, but the majority of the immigrants coming in today want nothing to do with becoming part of the American culture. They are more concerned about spreading their religion and culture upon us and are here to take advantage of the system we currently have in place. The Federation for American Immigration Reform estimates there are more than 425 thousand "anchor babies" (children born to illegal immigrants that are immediately granted U.S. citizenship) born in the U.S. each year. These births cost Medicaid an estimated $34.5 million dollars, the federal government $9.5 million dollars and taxpayers $31.3 million dollars, that's over seventy five million dollars spent in one hospital, in one city, in one border state.

The more immigrants that come into our country, the more democratic America becomes. So why should most immigrants support a Republican party that will cut taxes they do not pay rather than a Democratic party that will grow the programs on which they depend. Of our adult immigrants 31% never finish high school; the poverty rate is 57% higher than native-born Americans, and a third of all immigrants lack health care.

Only when the immigrants achieve economic security and a share of prosperity do they migrate toward the GOP, and this process usually takes generations. Mass immigration pushes politics to the left. If the GOP does not do something about immigration, immigration will do something about the GOP. Immigrants will be welcomed with open arms if they mean to become citizens and patriots as I'm sure there are some immigrants that will be, but all others need not apply.

<u>Are People still vacationing in Mexico?</u>

Police in the Mexican state of Veracruz said they have found the bodies of five men who were shot to death after being tortured, Veracruz state prosecutors said police found the men Tuesday April 05, 2011 on an empty lot. U.S. Drug Enforcement Administration said the U.S. worries about the spread of the Zetas cartel accused of killing a U.S. immigration agent in February and massacring 72 migrants in northern Mexico last year. This was announced after the killing of two U.S. citizens, waiting in line to reach the Tijuana border on Monday.

Wait there's more….Mexican security forces searching for abducted bus passengers in a violent state bordering Texas have stumbled on a collection of pits holding a total of 77 bodies. Authorities said the first victims identified are Mexicans, not migrants from other countries headed to the U.S.

It seems as though migrants in Mexico get turned into sex slaves. The Honduran consul in Mexico's southern Chiapas state, Patricia Villamil reported that young female migrants from Honduras and Guatemala are being tricked into making the dangerous journey across Central America in the hope for a better life. Only to be stopped en route in southern Mexico and forced to work for nothing as sex slaves…… The wave of drug-related killings which has claimed more than 37,000 thousand lives in just five years since the government launched an offensive against drug cartels - -drew thousands of protesters into the streets of Mexico's Capital. The State Department noted that 111 Americans were reported murdered in Mexico last year alone. You know it's sad when instead of taking care of the border problem, they issue a travel advisory warning us to stay away from southern Arizona and Texas. Wow I guess I better cancel my trip to Cancun this summer, and it was really cheap.

<u>Things Getting Worse?</u>

And if high unemployment, huge government deficits, rising gas/food prices and the weak housing market were not bad enough, now energy prices are surging because of the unrest and our new involvement in a possible third-war in the Middle East (Libya), and global supply chains have been disrupted by the disaster in Japan. Now we are dealing with inflation and the possibility of hyperinflation. Hyperinflation is not inflation on steroids, it is something entirely different. As inflation is the rising prices of goods and services, hyperinflation is the loss of faith in the U.S. currency. Prices rise in a hyperinflationary environment just like an inflationary one, but they rise not because people want more money for their labor or commodities, but because people are trying to get out of the currency. So they will pay anything for a good which is not the currency (look at the recent gold/silver boom).

Imagine being in a scenario without the ability to pump or afford gas, communicate, buy food, get medical care, or receive protection from law enforcement. You will have to rely on your own resources for God knows how long. Here is a basic checklist that I think will come in handy for all of us. If nothing else it will help put us in the right frame of mind when things get worse. This is a basic checklist and I highly advise you to add your own flavor to this as it pertains to you and your family.

Prepare for the Worse Checklist

* Save as much as you can, live within your means to have instant savings.
* Do you have a plan when and if things breakdown? (land, garden)
* Have backup plans – Most of us are all a crisis away from hard times, get ready.
* Stay liquid – If money is worthless or inaccessible it will not be a shock to you.
* Do you have a grab & go bag?
* Do you have cash/assets for buying or trading for goods?
* Do you have a gun & sufficient ammo?
* Invest in solar items such as radios to keep up on the news. Stock food, bottle water, medicine, and (cater to your family needs)
* Get smarter – continue to educate yourself on the issues, news, events, and keep family and friends informed. The more people that are awake around you the better off you will be.
* Wait (be patient) – Drive that older car longer, hold off buying that new home or taking that expensive vacation one more year. Also be prepared for inflation when the economy strengthens, especially in food and gas. Store can goods and bottle water.

Blogs in relation to this Chapter (We the People have Spoken)

- *I went from a shotgun to two semi-auto handguns and a concealed carry permit. Our country seems to be in greater peril on a daily basis, self-protection is very high on my survival list. I suggest you follow my lead.*

- *If you cannot feel the tension building throughout the world you live under a rock. Step away from the American media and take a look at International reports to gain a frightening look at what is happening in the rest of the world. Apart from natural disasters (floods/earthquakes) leaving millions destitute, diseased, and ever more angry I am seeing an increase in xenophobia. What really scares me is Germany starting publicly for the first time since WWII assert its desire to maintain its roots by saying that it made a mistake with foreign guest workers. Theo Sarazin's Hitler like views are being embraced far and wide, Budapest Hungary is creating neo Nazi youth hit squads and slowly starting to attack Jewish citizens. France is following with its attempt to kick out immigrants. Italians are attacking anyone darker than a paper bag. Now let us add currency wars, protectionism/tariffs. Much worse things are coming than foreclosures and short sales.*

- *The American Dream is only for rich people, the rest of us live the American Nightmare.*

- *Money is the root of all evil, if you have none and no marketable skills to acquire it. Acquire the skills people are willing to pay for and NEVER feel sorry for yourself. There is no free lunch in this world. Remember, whatever the government gives it can take away.*

- *I don't have a crystal ball or a magic mirror- but I see a sea of bankruptcy, depression (emotional and financial) - high unemployment for the next decade or longer.*

- *OBAMA = Civil War!!!*

- *Never, ever, ever, let them take your guns. For the blood of tyrants and patriots must be spilled from time to time to refresh the tree of liberty.*

- *Mexico is lost. Too much corruption in government and law enforcement to ever solve the problem. Decapitating, skinning people, these animals are worse than the ones in the Middle East. If I had to live in a border state I'd be building myself an arsenal. Is it going to have to reach Dallas before we do something about this?*

- *Watch out America (couch potatoes living in candy land) Shariah law is coming under freedom of religion! Our legislators will open the door to Hell in America - - Shariah law - -Freedom of religion.*

- *It's sad! I'm from Germany and we have even more problems with Islamstation, but to put a show off mosque on a sacred place is sick. God Bless you all!*

- *Mexico is such a screwed up country....we really need to secure our southern borders better and keep those folks out.*

- *What happens in Mexico stays in Mexico, including your dead body. I won't be back any time soon!!*

- *Seal the borders!!! We need to make every effort to keep those involved and that kind of terror out of the USA. Allowing illegals to enter our country is a dereliction of duty by our government.*

- *Unless the power elite wake up soon there will be big changes coming. The average people are waking up and realizing just how bad we have been screwed. Get yourself some land, stock your shelves, buy a few guns and guard dogs, learn how to grow food and be self-sufficient.*

- Oh yes, think of your grandchildren – they will live with this Islamic law or speak Chinese. These people are playing our game – and they intend to win. They have the will and the force to make it so. With the government we have (Godless & Constitution less) it will be an easy victory for them.

- I'm sorry to say this but, I believe the shit is going to hit the fan very soon. Americans like me are only going to take so much before we lock and load.

- No way in hell will I allow Shariah law in my country. I am a free woman and I will die a free woman.

- Muslims who want this country to be their home should comply with our laws, our Constitution, and pledge allegiance to our flag or get the hell out of our country!!

- So, under the current administration there are places in Mexico we cannot go to and places in our own country we cannot go to. What else will Obama give away to make foreigners happy?

- What a bunch of idiots we have in D.C. we can fight two, soon to be three wars overseas, yet we cannot secure our own borders…There's no excuse for it…We have been heading in a sickening direction for years…One day it will all come to a head and it will not be pretty for "we the people".

- If things keep going the way they are, guns and ammo will become the new currency.

- When the shit hits the fan, those decrying firearms will be hiding behind gun owners for protection and whimpering like babies. Talk *about outstanding investments. Politicians beware about attacking troops and law enforcement rights and benefits.*

IV

Age old Question (How do I become rich?)

"The Constitution guarantees you the pursuit of happiness, but it doesn't guarantee to finance the chase"
-Anonymous
"If you don't act like your poor, pretty soon you will be"
-Ron Martin

If there is one observation that I have noticed during my 40 plus years on this planet is that most people want to remain poor, and they do. What most people don't realize is that the road to wealth is paved with the ownership of things – real estate, businesses, equities, and the like. It takes hard work, sacrifice, and living a frugal life until the goal is reached. But the easiest and simplest way to accumulate income is to live within your means. Living within your means immediately generates some kind of savings, and with that income you can begin to build wealth. Since the "Great Recession" millions of people have become pessimistic. They have lost faith in the future and believe that things just will not work out. So they tend to squirrel money away into what they feel to be safe places such as local savings accounts and even in their own homes. With the interest rates being so low there is not much difference between the two. Most Americans don't believe their wages will increase or that their home prices will rise, nor do they believe it is a good to invest in anything but themselves.

On the other hand is the optimist who is always looking for opportunities to get rich quick and usually tends to takes things a little too far. They think they can invest in the stock market and pick the market winners or borrow fifty thousand dollars from the bank and double it on a get rich scheme. Our decisions about money should be based on our values, on our most important aspirations and on what we want to achieve in our lives. Because of our social mobility and social networking we encounter people on a daily basis who earn much more and much less than us.

But we never really know the financial circumstances behind someone's appearance. We don't know if someone has a trust fund, got really lucky in the stock market, has maxed-out the equity on their home, or is swimming in a sea of debt. A recent survey about America's financial literacy shows that most people don't know the difference between a stock and a bond, but realize they need to save money. They also admit that they don't know much about finance, and that they tend to spend money on things not needed rather than putting the money towards some kind of retirement savings. Financial ignorance plus missed opportunity spells disaster.

You see a lot of Americans living for the now without a care in the world about retirement. They vacation a few times a year, buy a new car every three or four years, and have all the new adult toys as soon as they come out. When they get closer to retirement age, they start to panic and realize that they will not have enough to retire on. In most cases retirement for American's is a dream deferred or not obtainable any more. I will attempt to educate you on the basics of finance for survival purposes only. Oh yeah I will explain the difference between a stock and a bond.

Bonds – Simply put bonds are loans. When a corporation wishes to build a plant or finance equipment purchases, it does so by floating a bond issue. Issuing bonds are less burdensome than those involved in issuing stock. Bonds are issued and traded in 1k dollar denominations and quoted in terms of "par" (100). So if a bond is quoted at 98 sells at $980, one quoted at 101 ½ sells at $1,015 and so on. Interest rates on bonds are fixed, so pay close attention to that fact. Bonds have appeal, despite their tendency to fluctuate in price as interest rates change, because they offer better defensive qualities than stocks. Also unlike stocks no bond can be put away and forgotten. Bonds should be watched closely. If you choose to add bonds to your investment plan, you have to remain alert and ready to shift positions according to your perception of overall interest rates and bond market trends.

Stocks – Short of diamonds, gold, silver, art, or some other esoteric storehouse of value, there's not much left in the way of choices for the saver but common stocks. Stocks always go up and down in value, sometimes with alarming speed, and sometimes to zero and disappear. There is, of course, more risk involved with a common stock than say, a bond, but the risk can be reduced by choosing stocks that have exhibited steady and dependable earnings and dividend growth over the years. The key is to look at the history of the stock. Is there a history of long dividend payments? What has the dividend growth been like? What is the stock's price-earnings ratio? Look for a strong steady business to invest in that has steady growth. It is a good rule of thumb to choose steady stocks and ride them out. It has been a fact that after every known recession stocks have rebounded 7% - 9%, not bad considering an average savings account sits at about 0.22% interest. We all heard about the people who lost everything in the great crash of 1929. Few of us hear about the solid investment gains enjoyed by thousands upon thousands of sensible buyers of good common stock. I will take it a step further a give you some stock picks that have done good by me over the last several years.

Sirius/XM Radio	Cisco	Renesola Ltd
Town Bank	Intel Corp.	Clean Energy Fuels Corp
Aurizon Mines	Smith & Wessson	Ebay

Average stock market returns since 1926 to present have been 9.6% for big company stocks and 11.67% for small company stocks. Stocks rarely hit this average in any given year. Instead prices tend to rise and fall like a rollercoaster ride, scaring the hell out of the faint of heart, and those who don't understand why they are investing. That is why it is not wise to invest short-term money into stocks. The job of the day-trader is essentially over. Stocks are so unpredictable and volatile in today's shaky economy and all the events happening in the Middle East, it is now best to pick strong companies and buy and hold and over the long run the rewarding upswings should equal the percentages mentioned above.

Saving and investing wisely is not an easy achievement, if it were we would all be rich. And in my forty plus years on this planet I personally do not know anyone who just fell into money. Their money was earned by working long hours and sacrificing to get where they are now. So I will make this as simple as I can for you. Act like your poor. Save as much as possible, as soon as possible. You will need to sacrifice your spending early in order to have a better chance of living the way you want when you want. Earn as much as possible as quickly as possible. Work more hours, take an additional job or two while you can and your mind and body lets you. Unless you are already living in poverty or real close to it, then it is possible for everyone to save something. Cut the cable off, go out to dinner less, pack your lunch and drink water from a fountain, wait for that movie to come out on DVD instead of paying theater prices, and many more sacrifices I don't think I have to list them all. Here is a list of things that you should stop paying for:

Things you should never pay for

1. Movies – wait until it comes out on DVD or TV
2. Newspapers – Read your news online
3. Coffee/water – make your own at the house and use the water fountain at work
4. Eating out – pack your lunch and cut-back drastically on eating out for dinner
5. Brokers – manage you own finance, unless you're a millionaire
6. Advice – this is something that most people will give for free
7. Firewood – cut your own
8. Pets – go to a shelter or adopt. Pass on the $1800 pet
9. Cell Phones – all carriers have a few free cell phones included in contract. Or just get the pay as you go phone from Wal-Mart or other retailers.
10. Exercise (gym memberships) – you can get all the exercise you need without paying those expensive gym fee and contracts.

You will have to resist the temptation of spending and creating debt. Social comparison, envy, and status-seeking have been part of the human condition since Cain and Abel. Keeping up with the Jones's will keep you in debt. According to the authors of *The Millionaire Next Door*, we all fall into one of three categories of wealth accumulation. There is the prodigious or in layman's terms over accumulator of wealth (PAW). They are the builders of wealth; they are the best at building net worth in comparison to others in their income/age bracket. Next are the average accumulator's of wealth (AAW), this where a good portion of us tend to dwell in. I say us because this is where I see myself right now. AAW's save and invest, not as much as we should or could, but we like to have fun and enjoy life also. Most AAW's have a tendency of thinking that we cannot take it with us, so we should try and enjoy life but not at the expense of not at least glimpsing in the future and having some sort of investments. Lastly there are the under accumulators of wealth (UAW). This is where the American majority resides for one reason or another. UAW's tend to live above their means; they emphasize consumption, and they tend to deemphasize many of the key factors that underlie wealth building. In short, they never consider their tomorrow.

You should evaluate yourself and determine which type of wealth accumulator you are. If you are a UAW and would like to become a PAW it isn't going to be easy. You generally have to be frugal and act and live like your poor, put off the new car, boat, and camper, pack your own lunch, and cut back on dining out. I actually found out that I was spending almost $900 dollars a month on lunch, dining out, and entertainment. That is almost another mortgage payment. You may have to move out of that glamorous neighborhood and move to a less costly area that will enable you to invest more of your income. You will pay less for your home and correspondingly less for your property taxes. Your neighbors will be less likely to drive expensive cars. You will find it easier to keep up, even stay ahead of the Joneses and still accumulate wealth. You have to continuously monitor your spending habits and make that change through self-talk and discipline. Here is a handy chart that will hopefully get you in the right mindset for reducing debt and keeping it down.

Debt	Saving
Leads to depression	Is rewarding
Becomes a habit	Should become a habit
Provides false security	Provides real security
Creates Stress	Reduces stress
Diminishes dignity	Re-enforces dignity

Once you have prioritized your debt, now it's time to put your plan to action. The biggest obstacle is getting and staying ahead. There are thousands of suggestions, tips, and tricks on how to do so, but let us start with trying the spending fast plan for a year. Spend only out of necessity and cut back as much as you can without foregoing the things you need and some wants. Track your savings and track the things that you are cutting back on, putting it on paper will help you stick to your goal and you can always revert back to it if need be.

There are not too many options to grow your money nowadays, with the interest rates being the lowest they have been in many years (see figure 2.) it's almost a crap shoot. As a matter of fact my online savings account that I opened at 5.3% in 2003 just sank to 0.80 last month. The interest rates for 5 May 2011 were 0.09, just a little bit better than my mattress. But I suggest you take the savings and invest it in the best venue at the time to grow to its maximum potential. Choose credit cards with the best rewards that work for you (ie. Cash back) and pay the balance off monthly to beat the interest rate. Use pre-paid cell phones to keep yourself within your minutes and no contracts that can be costly. If you cannot live without the cable, then use bundle services and make it a point to call your providers to see if there is any other applicable discounts that can be applied to keep your bill down as low as you can get it. The same goes for all your bills, do a monthly evaluation and see if there are ways to trim or get rid of services you no longer need.

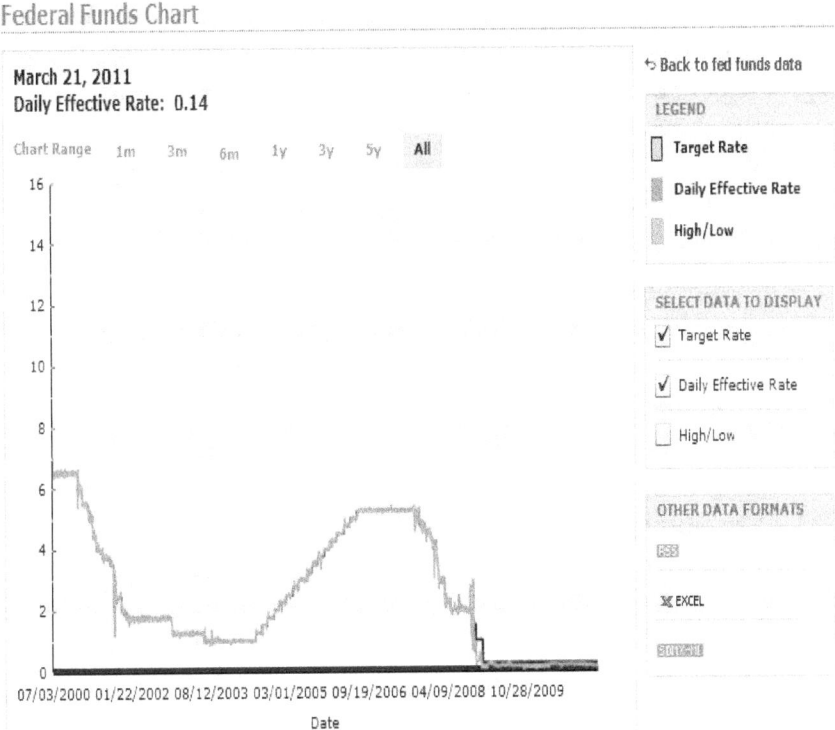

Figure 2

Most experts say you should save at least 10% of your monthly income to be able to retire comfortably. For most of us that goal seems pretty lofty, so it should be as much as you can. Another interesting stat I came across showed that us as Americans are only third in the world when it comes to saving and investing at around six percent. The Germans save around twenty percent of their income and the Swedish save around thirteen percent of theirs. So if we are the wealthiest nation in the world, we are a world of UAW's.

The goal is to have a safety net of at least six months' worth of income stashed away for emergencies due to the current average length of time spent without a job is thirty five and a half weeks. If you are fortunate enough to have a job that offers a 401k with any kind of match, I suggest that you maximize it now. Thirty-nine percent of 401k participants don't do so. Refusing to maximize your 401k is like telling your company you are not interested in extra money. Sure you have to contribute a little extra money per

85

paycheck, but this becomes savings – something we all need and will be able to rely on one day. Also remember that the money comes out of your check before it is taxed, so the damage is minimal, and the amount invested comes off the gross earnings reducing the income tax withholdings, thereby reducing the actual amount deducted from the paycheck by a couple of percent.

It has been said that we don't reach our age of financial reasoning until age 53, and falls sharply in the ages of 70's and 80's. I believe for most of us that is too late; we need to start now, by educating yourself and making it a habit in your daily life. I hear all too often people complaining about being broke, but refuse to do anything about it. The liberals preach re-distribution of wealth (as long as it's not their wealth) and the rich and affluent continue to be looked upon as the evil tyrants of this country.

When I was younger, my parents use to take us for a ride into the rich neighborhoods to see all the beautiful Christmas lights and decorations each year. We would look out the window in awe and hope that someday we would be able to have something close to that. The truth of the matter is that we can. Each and every one of us are given that opportunity to live like that, it's up to you whether or not you can. The sky is the limit in this country and we should all be thankful for that fact. Our decisions about money should be based on our values, on our most important aspirations, on what we want to achieve in our lives - - and then it's all about priorities.

The argument was made that if we took all the money in this country and put it in one big pot and distributed it all evenly to every man, woman, and child, most of us would be in the same situation in about two or three years. The reason is that people's mind sets won't change. Savers will still be savers, entrepreneurs and the business minded people will save and invest their money wisely and make it grow. The UAW's will spend their money and spend it quickly with having virtually nothing to show for it (except for a lot of pictures of the fun they had). The AAW's will do alright and probably be able to retire comfortably. But the PAW's will take their share, double and most likely triple it to become rich and hated again.

In a not so Perfect World

Now, I want to talk about worst case scenarios. Everything I have mentioned and talked about is great financial information in a stable economy. We are very far away from that and if things continue to get worse, we will have to be prepared when things do not get any better. Most people have lost their jobs, homes, savings, 401ks, and virtually left with nothing. I have friends and family members that are included in this scenario and just staying alive is what they are most concerned about, not becoming rich. If you have been fortunate enough to have kept your job and savings intact, you are definitely one of the few lucky ones. With land and real estate at an all-time low, you can still find great deals on raw land that you can buy and build on. Remember God is making more people but he isn't making any more land. None of us can predict the future, but we can see the writing on the wall by staying current in the news and many other channels via the internet and blogs. For instance you can tell Americans are panicking by watching the price of gold and silver rise beyond their all-time levels almost daily.

When the federal government made an announcement in a recent issue of the Navy Times and Federal Times about how they can borrow from your Thrift Savings Plan (TSP) in case of emergencies many of us came to a realization that nothing is safe. The government could temporarily tap tens of billions of dollars from two federal employee retirement programs if Congress fails to raise the debt ceiling next month, Treasury Secretary Timothy Geithner told lawmakers. The government expects to hit the $14.3 trillion dollar debt ceiling on 16 May or sooner. Congress expects to extend the debt ceiling by the deadline and said if it does not, Treasury will be forced to borrow money from the Civil Service Retirement and Disability Fund and the Thrift Savings Plan Investment Fund. These two moves could free up $142 billion dollars through July. By law, both funds have to be repaid with interest, said Susan Irving, director for federal budget analysis at the Government Accountability Office. Once these measures are

exhausted, the government will be limited in its ability to make payments across the government. If that were to happen, these issues would be the least of our worries, because we will face a worldwide economic collapse (are you feeling better now?).
I mean the government has been borrowing from Social Security for years and left a huge stack of IOUs in the pot. You cannot spend IOUs. So I'm sending a warning, do not be oblivious to what's going around you, stay awake and be prepared to make some moves when you have to.

Can Money buy Happiness?

Can money buy happiness? This has been one of the biggest financial questions of all-time. Numerous studies have shown that money does buy happiness...to a point. To the extent that money allows you to provide for your basic needs plus a little wiggle room, it does make you happier. The most recent study of this issue was published in the Proceedings of the National Academy of Sciences and found that a household income of $75k, money does nothing for happiness, enjoyment, sadness, or stress. Here is a list that correlates to happiness:

*   At least $75k
*   Spending money on other people and charity
*   Spending money on experiences over material goods
*   Living close to your job
*   Being older
*   Having a satisfying job
*   Strong social ties
*   Regular, monogamous sex

So you may be wasting your time:

*   Trying to be extremely wealthy
*   Wishing you were back in your 20s
*   Buying a bunch of junk

*   Enduring a lengthy commute to your job so you can have a bigger house

*   Involuntary celibacy

When people were asked what gives them the most pleasure, people favored health and home over stuff. If money can make the things on this list a reality, then yes I guess it can. Here is the list:

1. 84%   Good health
2. 60%   A home you own
3. 48%   Children
4. 46%   An interesting job
5. 36%   Free and leisure time
6. 22%   A yard or garden
7. 19%   A luxury or second car
8. 19%   The latest electronic gadgets

In the end though, happiness and being rich comes down to attitude and taking pleasure in the small things in life. I've known people who worked crappy jobs in deadbeat towns and still led happy lives. They learned to enjoy life's pleasures such as a good book, delicious food, and the beauty and refreshment of the outdoors. Instead of focusing on what they didn't have, these people focused on all the things they had going for them and fostered an attitude for gratitude.

So what does being rich really mean? A man once told me that it is when you lose your job; you will not have to work anymore. I guess that is a good definition, but to me it means something different indeed and it should to you also.

Blogs in relation to this Chapter (We the People have Spoken)

- *In America YOU choose what class YOU want to be part of/live within. No one is holding you back from achieving greatness except for YOU!!!*
- *If you don't get it yet…you will be in for a rude awakening, when you come up for air and all your wealth real or false is gone.*

- *Ok…go to the bank and open a savings account, checking account, money market account, and a CD. Please let me know how much interest the bank is going to pay you to bank with them. There's no money there, so what alternatives do we have now?*

- *The point is not to become a millionaire. It is to become free. Once you know you have enough to keep a roof over your head and food on the table, now you can make choices about what you want to do; where you want to live; how you want the rest of your life to play out.*

- *Oh look! The stock market ended on a high at the end of the day…..Like it always does. Not one more of my hardworking dollars will ever go to the Wall Street crooks ever again.*

- *Much of the credit and housing bubble was due to people buying things they couldn't afford; taking out equity lines for a 4th Lexus on ½ million dollar home. Now the plan is to do it all over again. This should end well….*

- *No one can feed their families on minimum wage. It was meant to be a stepping stone not a career.*

- *Main street people often do not own stocks, so higher gas and food prices will only make us feel poorer not richer.*

- *Idiots spending money they don't have while defaulting on mortgages, complaining and barely affording food and fuel every week, and not saving a penny, but spending next week's paycheck before they earned it to ease the commercial pressures of happiness on a materialistic ritual known as a holiday. A holiday for the average American family would be a break from bills. Do yourselves a favor spend less or not at all, you will be a lot happier and it will make for a better New Year.*

- *Social Security was also a "Trust Fund". Look what happened to that. I would not put anything past the members of Congress.*

- *Your 401k isn't safe either, what the stock market casino doesn't eat up the government will confiscate when it goes over the cliff, and the cliff is approaching rapidly.*

- *Save as much as possible or you'll be screwed. I don't make a ton of money, but I save a lot. I drive an old crappy car, I do a lot of free activities and have a lot of fun playing outside with my three sons. Less stuff will make you happier, not more stuff.*

- *If you came here legally I would love to help you, if you didn't then I don't feel sorry nor do I want to spend another hour of my day working for your free benefits and aid. Go back to where you came from and apply legally like my family did.*

V

Politics & Religion

"The God who gave us life gave us liberty at the same time"
-Thomas Jefferson

Politics and religion has always been a subject of conversation that I shied away from, unless it was with close friends around a campfire. Anyone of these subjects can become so heated that it makes most people want to fight or un-friend someone. Being someone that has studied the Christian faith and truly believes in God and all of his glory, I will give testimony to someone that I feel is asking me for it or is just curious and doesn't really know what to believe in yet. Then and only then will I project my views. The same goes for politics. I have my own opinions and my own believes and only recently have felt comfortable telling my side and interjecting my views.

This country has taken a turn for the worse and it is time for all of us to get off the side lines and start speaking our minds and projecting our views so the millions of people out there that really don't care or know can formulate their own opinions and voice their own views. We have all been silent too long and now the government is taken control of almost everything we hold dear to us. The Founding fathers are turning over in their graves right now as we as a country have strayed from the Constitution and religion.

The English established colonies along the east coast of North America, but by mid 1700s, the military and economic interests of the Americans were no longer compatible with those of the English. After King George III increased taxes in America to pay for his European wars, the resulting riots and rebellious actions throughout the American colonies forced the King to tighten his grip on power until the oppression became intolerable. Thomas Paine called for Americans to declare their independence and establish a democratic government based on freedom and equality. Thomas Paine's writing of the radical pamphlet called "Common Sense" converted hundreds of thousands of Americans to the cause. During the War of Independence, the American States began experimenting with democracy.

There was an immediate concern among the wealth of the minority. Several years after winning the War of Independence, a national convention was held to draft a constitution for the United States of America. Using the English system of government as a model, with a congress of regional representatives, a senate of state representatives, and an elected President instead of a King, they created a balanced democratic system in which each new law would need to pass through three levels of government before being interpreted by the courts. The three levels of the United States government include the Executive Branch (President and his cabinet), the Legislative Branch (Congress), and the Judicial Branch (Supreme Court).

The United States was founded in 1787 when the constitution became the supreme law of the land. The new constitution seemed to favor wealthy landowners who had managed to secure most of the political power themselves. Over the next decade there was an intense political struggle to reform the constitution. The reform was led by Thomas Jefferson who eventually succeeded in amending the constitution to guarantee rights like freedom of speech, freedom of religion, and the right to keep and bear arms (my favorite).

Our founding fathers were statesmen. They were men of high integrity. Incredible wisdom, unquestionable faith and love of country that shared a common vision of creating a republic that would last through the ages. They saw beyond their own lives, in fact they put their lives and fortunes at risk to give birth to our country. The incredible bravery of these statesmen should never be forgotten or taken for granted by anyone who treasures liberty and freedom.

Religion has been a huge part of this country since its inception (235 years). The Bible was the one book that literate Americans in the seventeenth, eighteenth, and nineteenth centuries were expected to know. The Pilgrims believed in God, covenants, sin, and justice. Fifty six signers of the Declaration of Independence were mostly Christians and they represented a mostly Christian people. These are just some examples, and before we move on I will give one more.

When George Washington became commander of the Continental Army, he knew there would be hard winters and hot summers, with no pay and little food. He knew victories would be scarce – the men would have to become use to retreating, falling back, and evading, just to survive. Washington also knew his only hope lay in conviction in the hearts and daily actions of all his men that what they did for God, and under God's protection. Therefore, Washington gave orders that each day begin with formal prayer, to be led by the officers of each unit. Thus, on July 9, 1776 Chaplains were born. These were to be persons of good character that led exemplary lives. Washington would see that these men were respected by all, uniform officers and soldiers alike and would pay suitable respect and attend religious exercises led by these men.

Even today polls show that roughly 92 percent of Americans still believe in a creator. But what they perceive as a creator has changed over the years. Our religious beliefs are in flux. I mean one in four Americans has left the denominational faith in which they were raised. One in five claims no particular faith at all. And one in four young adults, between the ages of eighteen and twenty-nine is an atheist or agnostic. This is a far different picture from early

America, where Christianity and our republic were intricately intertwined.

Amid growing fear and anxiety, religious conservatives are gaining political power around the world. They do not want their children growing up without hope for the future, to become another generation whose only sense of self-worth is their physical appearance or their possessions, and whose only purpose is to stimulate the pleasure centers in the brain. They don't want their children growing up to become too selfish, confused, and immature to be able to successfully raise their own families. Just take a look around, how many 20 – 30 something children do you see still living at home? It is becoming the norm.

People's ideas about right and wrong generally reflect their own selfish interests or the interests of the group they belong to. When the struggle for power is not restrained by laws or morals, then whichever group gains power will usually try to further its own interests at the expense of everyone else's. Religious hostility was mostly confined to a few troubled regions where people with differing faiths shared the same area of land. Religious differences often fueled bitter power struggles for political control of the land, which occasionally erupted into violence and bloodshed.

Democratic politics is almost entirely driven by greed and self-interest. Each election is like a selfish grab for power. Political parties do whatever they can within the law to swing votes their way. People vote for the party that will tax them less, spend more on their personal interests, and bias the law in their favor. Democracy has succeeded over every other form of government because people have a peaceful way of removing leaders they no longer want. After being in politics too long even the honest politicians tend to become corrupted by power and greed. Winston Churchill once said that Democracy is the worst form of government on earth, but compared to the rest, it is still the best. James Madison wrote, "If men were angels, no government would be necessary. But since men are not angels, without government human beings would live in a state of nature, where the weaker individual is not secured against violence of the stronger".

The purpose of government is to enforce the natural law for the members of the political community by securing the people's natural rights. It does so by preserving their lives and liberties against violence of others. In the founding, the liberty to be secured by government is not freedom from necessity or poverty. It is freedom from the domination of some human beings over others. Now it seems that the government is involved in almost every facet of our lives. And yes here it is again, *a government that provides for everything is a government capable of taking everything.*

What we need is less government and more citizenship. If we let government takeover healthcare, now the government owns healthcare. If we let the government takeover housing, now the government owns the housing sector. In the two years' worth of research I have conducted, these are the number one concerns of Americans today:

1. Bring back jobs
2. Stop the spending and reduce the deficit
3. Clean up the housing fiasco
4. Protect our borders and deport illegal immigrants
5. Less government involvement in our daily lives
6. Term-Limits on Politicians

In a Bloomberg National Poll held on December 14, 2010, the public wants Congress to keep its hands off entitlements such as Medicare, Medicaid, and Social Security, and no increases in the gasoline tax. Americans want Congress to bring down the federal budget deficit under two conditions: minimize the pain and make the rich pay. Americans are in no mood for further hurt in a slow economy and high unemployment. The one place Americans are willing to sacrifice is in the wallets of the wealthy and Wall Street. They want tax cuts to end for the rich, and a tax reform to be put in place on Wall Street profits.

These and many more issues are on the minds of most Americans, but it will take every one of us to get off our butts and make our voices heard. Whether you are a Democrat liberal, or a

Republican conservative these issues involve us all. Speaking of the different parties and this being a layman's guide I will attempt to explain the differences just in case you don't fully know where you stand. The Democratic Party is often called "the party of Jefferson", while the modern Republican party is often called "the party of Lincoln".

These parties were organized by Thomas Jefferson and James Madison, and favored state's rights and strict adherence to the Constitution. Since the 1890s, the **Democratic Party** has favored liberal positions. Historically, the party has favored farmers, laborers, labor unions, and religious and ethnic minorities. The party began advocating welfare spending programs targeted at the poor. The **Republican ideology** was reflected in 1856 for free labor, free land, and free men. They favor fiscal conservatism and the promotion of personal responsibilities over welfare programs, believe private spending is more efficient than government spending and oppose the estate tax. Republicans also believe there should be a safety net to assist the less fortunate, and believe the private sector is more effective in helping the poor than the government is.

In a recent poll conducted in 2009 revealed that 53% of Americans believe capitalism is a better system than socialism, and 27% are "not sure". In our younger generation it's even scarier, 37% preferred capitalism, and 33% preferred socialism and a whopping 30% were undecided. I'm sure that the main reason for the undecided and the not sure were because they don't know the difference and are afraid to ask. So I will explain the difference for you (no more excuses).

Capitalism – is an economic system in which the means of production are privately owned and operated for a private profit; decisions regarding supply, demand, price, distribution, and investments are made by private actors in the free market; profit is distributed to owners who invest in business, and wages are paid to workers employed by businesses and companies.

Socialism – is an economic and political theory educating public or common ownership and cooperative management of the means of production and allocation of resources (in layman's terms if you have two and I have zero, you give me one, now we both have one). A socialist society is characterized by a free association, which is not based on coercive wage labor. It is organized on the basis of relatively equal power relations, self-management, collective decision-making and adhocracy rather than hierarchical, bureaucratic forms of organization in the economic and political systems.

If you are still wondering which party or parties you as an individual should favor go to the website http://www.gotoquiz.com/conservative_or_liberal and take a few minutes to complete the quiz. I scored 82% conservative, which says that I believe in personal responsibility, limited government; free markets, individual liberty, traditional American values and a strong national defense. I believe that the role of the government should be to provide people the freedom necessary to pursue their own goals. I will list the main issues confronting us as a country and show you where the two parties stand on each:

The Issues

Affirmative Action
Liberals: Due to prevalent racism in the past, minorities were deprived of the same education and employment opportunities as the whites. The government must work to make up for that. America as a society is still racist; therefore a federal affirmative action law is necessary.

Conservatives: Individuals should be admitted to schools and hired for jobs based on their ability. It is unfair to use race as a factor in the selection process. Reverse discrimination is not a solution for racism. Some individuals in society are racist, but American society as a whole is not. Preferential treatment of certain races through affirmative action is wrong.

Economy

Liberals: A market system in which government regulates the economy is best. Government must protect citizens from the greed of big business. Government regulation in all areas of the economy is needed to level the playing field.

Conservatives: The free market system, competitive capitalism, and private enterprise create the greatest opportunity and the highest standard of living for all. Free markets produce more economic growth, more jobs, and higher standards of living than those systems burdened by excessive government regulation.

Education

Liberals: Public schools are the best way to educate students. Vouchers take money away from public schools. Government should focus additional funds on existing public schools, raising teachers' salaries, and reducing class size.

Conservatives: School vouchers create competition and therefore encourage schools to improve performance. Vouchers will give all parents the right to choose good schools for their children, not just those who can afford private schools.

Gun Control

Liberals: The Second Amendment does not give citizens the right to keep and bear arms, but only allows for the state to keep a militia (National Guard). Individuals do not need guns for protection; it is the role of local and federal government to protect the people through law enforcement agencies and the military. Additional gun control laws are necessary to stop gun violence and limit the ability of criminals to obtain guns. More guns mean more violence.

Conservatives: The Second Amendment gives citizens the right to keep and bear arms. Individuals have the right to defend themselves. There are too many gun control laws—additional laws will not lower gun crime rates. What is needed is enforcement of current laws. Gun control laws do not prevent criminals from obtaining guns. More guns in the hands of law-abiding citizens mean less crime.

HealthCare

Liberals: Support free or low-cost government controlled healthcare. There are millions of Americans who can't afford healthcare and are deprived of this basic right. Every American has a right to affordable healthcare. The government should provide healthcare benefits for all, regardless of their ability to pay.

Conservatives: Support competitive; free market healthcare system. All Americans have access to healthcare. The debate is about who should pay for it. Free and low-cost government run programs result in higher costs and everyone receiving the same poor quality healthcare. Healthcare should remain privatized. The problem of uninsured individuals should be addressed and solved within the free market healthcare system—the government should not control healthcare.

Immigration

Liberals: Support legal immigration. Support blanket amnesty for those who enter the United States illegally. Also believe that illegals have a right to—all educational and healthcare benefits that citizens receive (financial aid, welfare, social security and Medicare), regardless of legal status. Illegals should have the same rights as American citizens, it's unfair to arrest and deport millions of illegal immigrants.

Conservatives: Support legal immigration. Oppose amnesty for those who enter illegally. Those who break the law do not have the same rights as those who obey the law and enter legally. The borders should be secured before addressing the problem of illegal immigration currently in the country. The federal government should secure the borders and enforce current immigration laws.

Private Property

Liberals: Government has the right to use eminent domain (seizure of private property by the government with compensation to the owner) to accomplish a public end.

Conservatives: Respect ownership and private property rights. Eminent domain in most cases is wrong. Eminent domain should not be used for private development.

Religion & Government

Liberals: Support the separation of Church and State. The Bill of Rights implies a separation of Church and State. Religious expression has no place in government and should not support religious expression in anyway. All reference to God in public and government spaces should be removed (eg. Ten Commandments should not be displayed in federal buildings).

Conservatives: The phrase "separation of Church and State" is not in the Constitution. The first Amendment to the Constitution states "Congress shall make no law respecting an establishment of religion, or prohibiting the free exercise thereof...." This prevents the government from establishing a national church/denomination. However, it does not prohibit God from being acknowledged in schools and government buildings.

Social Security:

Liberals: The Social Security system should be protected at all costs. Reduction in future benefits is not a reasonable option. Social Security provides a safety net for the nation's poor and needy. Changing the system would cause a reduction in benefits and many people would suffer as a result.

Conservatives: The Social Security system is in serious financial trouble. Major changes to the current system are in dire need. In its current state, the Social Security system is not financially sustainable. It will collapse if nothing is done to address the problems. Many will suffer as a result. Social Security must be made efficient through privatization and/ or allowing the individual to manage their own savings. Social Security should be an option not mandated like it is today.

Taxes

Liberals: Higher taxes (primarily for the wealthy) and a larger government are necessary to address inequity/injustice in society (government should help the poor and needy using tax dollars from the rich) Support a large government to create jobs and provide welfare programs for those in need. Government programs are a caring way to provide for the poor and needy in society.

Conservatives: Lower taxes and a smaller government with limited power will improve the standard of living for all. Support lower taxes and a smaller government. Lower taxes will create more incentive for people to work, save, invest, and engage in entrepreneurial endeavors. Money is best spent by those who earn it, not the government. Government programs encourage people to become dependent and lazy, rather than encouraging work and independence.

Welfare

Liberals: Support welfare, including long-term welfare. Welfare is a safety net which provides for the poor and needy. Welfare is necessary to bring fairness to American economic life. It is a device for protecting the poor.

Conservatives: Oppose long-term welfare. Opportunities should be provided to make possible for those in need to become self-reliant. It is for more compassionate and effective to encourage people to become self-reliant, rather than allowing them to remain dependent on the government for provisions.

As you can see the differences between the two are quit significant. Unfortunately we are not all equal. The American that gets up early and works late is not equal to the American that sleeps till noon and collects their so-called entitlements. Now looking at some of the issues I listed above, you as an individual have your own thoughts and should not be swayed either way. The point is that if you have a problem or a concern then it is solely up to you to do something about it. What can I do you say?

We are rapidly approaching the 2012 presidential elections and as the candidates start to make themselves known, research each candidate and vote for the one that you agree with. I have dedicated Chapter eight of my book in doing the research for you, to help you make the choice that is right for you and hopefully for our country. But don't just take my word for it, please do your own research and attend your community town hall meetings and make your voices heard. Write and email your Congressman or woman with your concerns and hold them accountable for the things they said they would do.

If you're pissed off about a certain issue, make it known to them. Politics, like religion is full of heretics and false prophets. If you do not know the Constitution of the United States and/ or the Bible, you will be easily led astray in both politics and religion. Both have and will continue to be misinterpreted by many (as we have seen a lot as of late). Corrupt politicians promise us an easy shortcut to the good life and now are making more false promises. They are telling us to throw money at the problems they have created and it will stop our countries out of control spiraling of debt. They want us to spend more of our hard earned dollars to "stimulate" the economy.

They have convinced us that the more we spend the faster we will recover. This is the definition of insanity. The conservative definition of the word insanity is doing the same thing over and over again expecting a different result (not going to happen). If We the People don't hold our government officials accountable for their actions, then God help us all when we have to explain to our children and grandchildren how we let this happen to our country while doing nothing…If we fail to speak up and speak out against the madness then we should be prepared to accept everything that comes our way.

The Tower of Babel (all over again)

There was a time in history according to the book of Genesis 11:1-9 when we all were of one language and one speech. As the people migrated from the east to the land of Shinar, they decided to build a great tower to reach the heavens. Building the tower wasn't the problem, the higher the tower became, the more evil the hearts of the people became. When God found out about their evil plan, he confounded their speech, confused their languages, and scattered them abroad the earth as a punishment for their disrespect. Not one of them could speak the same language or understand each other, hence the name "The Tower of Babel". Now that America is becoming a multicultural, multiethnic, and multilingual country it seems again we are being punished. We are no longer Protestant, Catholic, and Jews. We are Protestant, Catholic, Jew, Orthodox,

Mormon, Muslim, Hindu, Buddhist, Taoist, Shintoist, Santeria, voodoo, agnostic, atheist, humanist, Rastafarian, and Wiccan. If we do not again become one nation and one people under the same God, we will lose our country. And there is no greater sorrow on earth than the loss of one's native land.

It seems as we are waiting around for the next attack, possibly detonation of a nuclear bomb. And we watch helplessly as our politicians and religious leaders bumble their way through one world crisis after the next. Our world has a long history of political and religious extremists using violence to force their beliefs upon others. Even in the modern democratic world freedom of speech has become an almost sacred right, this freedom is far from assured when it comes to the matter of religion.

The Muslim Brotherhood is using two principles to push their religion: Taqiyya and Da'wa. The first is the Islamic practice of "concealing or disguising one's beliefs, convictions, ideas, feelings, opinions, and/or strategies at a time of eminent danger, to save oneself from physical and/or mental injury. Taqiyya is also used as justification for lies and deceit to advance the cause of Islam. Da'wa is the act of inviting non-Muslims to accept Islam. Performing Da'wa involves both words and actions, and is frequently practiced in public schools in America. Conversion is the ultimate goal on the part of the Muslim initiating Da'wa.

Here is my last thought on this chapter. In democratic countries, the growing numbers of unemployed will have the political power to demand higher welfare payments, free health care, affordable housing, and other government benefits and entitlements. The wealthy and well-to-do may not like having to pay for the permanently unemployed, but unless the growing numbers of unemployed can afford to be consumers, then the drop in demand will lead to a fall in production and the loss of even more jobs and the shrinking economy will spiral downwards into a developing depression. More government handouts and involvement in our lives is not the answer to our problems.

The entire world is going to have to change its way of thinking and become much more mature and responsible if we are going to have any chance of surviving the challenges ahead. In our brave new world many people who grow up and live in modern societies are now abandoning their traditional religious beliefs and adopting a more materialistic outlook on life. In the absence of any believable explanation for human existence, many now believe that there is nothing worth believing in, without any purpose or meaning to their lives, many are descending into despair and depression. Without any clear vision for the future of the world, nations are continuing to prepare for war (sad but true).

Who said it?

Now don't get me wrong, the people I meet in small towns and big cities, don't expect government to solve all their problems. They know they have to work hard to get ahead. And they want to. Go into blue collar counties around Chicago and people will tell you: They don't want their tax money wasted by a welfare agency or by the Pentagon. Go into any inner-city neighborhood, and folks will tell you that government alone can't teach kids to learn. They know that parents have to teach, that children can't achieve unless we raise their expectations and turn off the television set and eradicate the slander that says black youth with a book is acting white. They know those things.
Keynote speech in 2004 at the Democratic National Convention by Barack Obama (go figure).

Blogs in relation to this Chapter (We the People have Spoken)

- *Look to the Lord Jesus Christ and pray in faith. I'm in construction and there is very little work out there. My two sons worked for me and they as well had no work. Many of my co-workers who are at retirement age have lost everything because of the lack of work. So we can only turn to God to seek his will in our life right now and hope whatever he provides will bring glory to him. I will pray for you and may God's blessing be with you today and always.*
- *How did people live 75 years ago without the government taking charge? Did they learn to use knives and forks all by themselves? It's amazing.*

- *I think the best way to solve the differences over the two parties, is to have every citizen decide on what party they will follow, separate the money in two piles. It should be interesting to see who will do better in 10 years.*

- *Keep the country safe, protect my family and property, keep the dollar strong, create a policy environment in which the private sector can thrive and create jobs, and balance the budget. Otherwise, stay out of my life!!!!*

- *At what point do WE, the middle-class people of this country say enough is enough! Take care of the American people first! Leave the elderly Social Security alone; leave Medicare alone, it's all they have. Shames on us for letting our government do this to us. They need to realize that they work for us!!!!*

- *We can ask the government to solve all of our problems or we can tell them to butt out and let us manage our own lives. I prefer the latter!!!!!*

VI

The Most Respectable Job in America

"The object of war is not to die for your country, but to make the other bastard die for his"
-General George S. Patton
"All gave some, some gave all"
-Anonymous

My pastor once said that every man should have a respectable job. Those words stuck in my head for many years and still rings true today. I have often repeated those words to my children and young sailors that I mentored throughout my twenty two years in the military. When I heard those words I was on active duty in the U.S. Navy and I thought to myself that I could not be doing a job that I could feel more proud of doing. I think that being a military member has to be one of the most respectable jobs on the planet. Not to take anything away from our police officers, fire fighters, and school teachers. Our all-volunteer military has given us a motivated, highly professional fighting force. But it has created a warrior class distinct from the rest of society. Perhaps it has to be that way.

Seventy five percent of Americans ages 17 – 24 are unfit for military service. Most young Americans are physically unfit, and others have criminal records or inadequate educations. Another national study has found that thousands of students fail the military's entrance exam each year for one reason or another. The report shows that 23% of recent high school graduates do not get the minimum score needed on the enlistment test to join any branch of military service. Among those who can and do make the grade are Americans of military families. Military service tends to run in families, sometimes for generations. Family traditions serve the armed forces well, but they keep the burden of war within a narrow group. Lucky for us that this group doesn't mind the burden. They are ready to do what needs to be done to protect our freedom and liberties. They know how valuable they are to us because they have either seen it or been told by their parents, grandparents, aunts and uncles, and brothers and sisters.

I come from one of those families. My grandfather was in the Army, my dad was in the Army and served in Vietnam, I served in Operation Desert Storm, Operation Enduring Freedom, and Operation Iraqi Freedom, and my son joined the United States Navy in September 2008 serving abroad at the writing of this book. My wife has served in the United States Army, and her family is one of military tradition also, as my step-son is set to leave for Navy boot camp this year once he graduates high school.

Thank goodness that our veterans today usually receive only gratitude from civilians, unlike our brothers returning from Vietnam. That support means more than you know. A simple "thank you for your service" gives us goose bumps and a since of pride that runs deep within each one of us. That's why it's so important that the public acknowledges the sacrifices of our military personnel. Most American veterans view their military service and experiences as the highlight of their working lives. In the meantime, the United States remains involved in two major combat zones (Libya will be the third) and deployed around the world in many hostile countries. Tomorrow's veterans are training today. Please think of them and pray for them often and support them in any way you can.

History of the United States military evolved from a new nation fighting the British Empire for Independence without a professional military, to the world's sole remaining super power of the late twentieth century and early twenty first century. The Continental Army was created in 1775 and named George Washington as its commander. This newly formed army, along with state militia forces, and the French Army and Navy defeated the British in 1783. The military has been a vital part of our country since before it was considered our country, even to this day our brave and courageous men and women of the United States military make sacrifices that only those who have served could even imagine, to insure our freedom and liberties. The words "freedom isn't free" could not be any closer to the truth. It has been and still is being bought and paid for every day.

My Dad once said that our military is the police of the world. Every time someone farts we have to go over there and smell it. Just to give you an example of what I'm talking about here is a list of past and present wars and conflicts our great nation has been part of.

Colonial Wars	1620 – 1774	World War I	1917 – 1918
War of Independence	1775 – 1783	World War II	1939 – 1945
Early National Period	1783 – 1815	Cold War	1945 – 1991
Continental Expansion	1816 – 1860	Korean War	1950 – 1953
American Civil War	1861 – 1865	Vietnam War	1955 – 1975
Indian Wars	1865 – 1870	Grenada	1983
Spanish American War	1898	Panama	1989
Banana Wars	1898 – 1935	Gulf War	1990 – 1991

Somalia	1992 – 1994
War on Terrorism	2001 – Present
Opr Enduring Freedom	2001 – Present
Opr Iraqi Freedom	2003 – 2010

Our recent conflicts and wars have claimed the lives of more than 6,000 American soldiers and those numbers increase every day. The numbers of the wounded are over 36,650 and also rising. Don't be naive and think this trend will ever stop; it has been and will always be a part of who we are. We presently have troops in over 140 countries around the world. War has become big business for America, we not only consume a vast amount of military equipment but we sell it to the rest of the world. America is the largest exporter of weapons of all shapes and sizes in the world. So we will always need brave, committed, and honorable men and women to want to be part of the greatest military in the world for us to be successful as a nation.

We currently have one point five million active duty members in our Armed Forces, eight hundred fifty thousand in the reserve forces, and twenty three point five million veterans. Due to the current events in our country and the still high unemployment rate, the military has been almost filled to maximum capacity. The recruiters can only put in on average one active duty person per month. If you decide you would like to join after you graduate high school and you meet the criteria you will most likely have to wait and join the reserve forces until an active duty billet opens up.

The days of getting in the military service with a General Education Development (GED) are also over. There was a time when the military could put in at least 10% GEDs, but those days are gone and that is why I stress education so much in chapter one. The most effective and almost only way to go in active duty is to enlist as a high school senior and ship out sometime after you graduate with a diploma and a military contract.

The Troops really do need our Support

You see the bumper stickers, lapel pins, t-shirts, and bulletin boards everywhere you go with the slogan "Support our Troops". Now more than ever our troops really do need our support, so let's help the ones that risk their lives daily for us. The White House launched a national campaign to better assist military troops, veterans, and their families struggling with the aftermath of 10 years of war. Military assistance groups acknowledge the troops and their families continue to grapple with often-hidden wounds of war. These include not only the 43,000 troops who have sustained combat injuries, but also those who face financial pressures and children who are falling behind in school. These plights often go unacknowledged by much of the country, because less than one-percent of Americans serve in the United States armed forces.

The new White House initiative, called *Joining Forces*, will focus on improving employment opportunities, education, and mental health among troops and their families. Homelessness continues to plaque veterans as well. About one-third of adult homeless populations are veterans, according to the National Coalition for Homeless Veterans. The Veteran's Administration estimates that 107,000 veterans nationwide are homeless on any given night. These great Americans who have risk their lives for our freedoms and liberties, so that we could sleep in our beds at night without worry, do not have a bed of their own that they can lay in. That is insane. You can learn more and help by visiting the following website at: http://www.va.gov/HOMELESS/index.asp

Much of the stress placed on troops and their families is the result of the rapid pace of deployments over the past ten years. Over 2.2 million U.S troops have deployed during that time, some 800,000 troops have served multiple tours, including twenty-five percent who have gone to war three or more times. These deployments create stress and financial strain for spouses as well, who have a more difficult time holding down jobs because of the frequent moves among military families and the need to care for children while the other spouse is fighting a war.

I have been part of the above mentioned group of service members who have been involved in multiple wars and conflicts. The strain on each family member cannot be fathomed by the normal American unless they have been part of the situation in some way. In my twenty-two years of service my children have lived the majority of their school-aged lives without me being around much and my marriage ended after twenty years of strain and stress.

Military life is tough for service members, spouses, and children. But in my opinion the children seem to have the most difficult time adapting to the transition. They can spend the majority of their lives moving from place-to-place, city-to-city, or country-to-country. They can possibly change schools three or more times in a single school year. Imagine being twelve years old, finally making friends and having to pack up and move to a different country. These changes can be more traumatizing for older children when their friends and finding their identity is (to them) the most important aspect of their young lives.

I have seen situations where children would live with relatives as the service member served overseas just to be able to stay in school in the United States. So most military member's families, down to the long lost Aunt or Uncle may be involved in the process of taking care of children and sometimes spouses at some point during the military member's career. That is why good strong family support is very much needed in contributing to the success of the military member. Because believe me when things are not right at home, no matter where the service member is his/her mind will not be 100% committed to their job or mission and that could be fatal to a lot of people.

Why is America not hiring Veterans?

Iraq and Afghanistan veterans are meeting with members of Congress and the Obama administration to urge that everyone commit to reducing veterans unemployment. Their goal is to reduce the veteran's unemployment rate to at least match the national unemployment rate by Veterans Day. The Labor Department reported that in 2010, the unemployment rate for Iraq and Afghanistan-era veterans was 11.5% while the unemployment rate for nonveterans was 9.7%. Since the start of 2011, the unemployment rate for veterans has been even higher - -15.2% in January and 12.5% in February.

The reality is, as the government continues to reduce our troop end strength, more veterans will be looking for civilian employment. Among the problems cited by veterans groups is that skills a service member acquires in the military do not always transfer to the civilian world. I mentioned this is chapter one's "*The art of resume writing*" section that you have to be the one to make sure that the conversion of your military skill-set is translated to the civilian equivalent. Even though most of your military schools and certifications will not convert over you can use the on-the-job training portion to your advantage. The other problem is that a lot of private sector employers are skeptical of hiring Iraq and Afghanistan-era veterans because they have spent so much time in the sand. They perceive them to be mentally unstable and loose cannons. I think the exact opposite is true. These veterans are very mentally stable, hardworking, and trained leaders that would be a great asset to any company that is lucky enough to have them.

President Obama signed an executive order in late 2009, creating a council representing 24 agencies devoted to recruiting and hiring veterans. They want to ensure that at least 27% of new hires in fiscal year 2010 were veterans. Ray Jefferson, assistant secretary for veteran's employment and training at the Labor Department says the program that helps train veterans for civilian jobs may have lost its luster over the years. He and his staff members are in the process of revamping the program, known as the Transition Assistance Program (TAP).

I participated in TAP about three years ago and it very was helpful. The class was a week long and its main focus was to assist the veteran in transitioning to the civilian sector. They assisted with resume writing and had representatives from real employers conducting mock interviews. They even had two representatives from S&K men's suits to show us how to dress for interviews. But since the "Great Recession" things have changed drastically. Veterans with less than marketable rates (jobs), have a harder time than those that were in say the IT field. I do agree with embedding a better system to help convert military schools, and training to the civilian sector. I also suggest to service members to do all you can to continuously build your worth. If you are in a rate/job that you know is not in very high-demand in the civilian world, then get a degree and/or certifications in a field that is. Your education is being paid for; it only requires your time and effort. Do not put the responsibility of your life and or career in someone else's hands.

Brigette Gabriel, in her book *They Must Be Stopped* had a note of thanks to the military in the back of her book that I wanted to include in this chapter. I really hope that every that reads my book will have a chance to read hers as well.

"Words tremble on my lips and emotions swell in my heart in my attempt to humbly thank you for all the things you do to protect America and the world. Words cannot express my depth of gratitude to your service, to your sacrifice, to all that you leave behind to go forth into the world and protect America's interests around the globe.

Let my grateful tears thank you for the nights you slept freezing in a tent or sweating in the desert, for the lonely days you spent missing your loved ones, for the hours you spent sick in pain and without someone holding your hand, for the moments of sheer fright in the heart of battle, for the wounds you suffered fighting evil, for the endless days in the hospitals undergoing painful surgeries, for the precious occasions you have missed back home.

For all of the sacrifices I thank you. We truly appreciate these sacrifices.

A special thank-you is in order to your families, to the parents who raised you and made you be the man or woman you are today. I thank your wives, husbands, and your loved ones who stand by you and support you with their love and dedication.

And for those who returned in eternal sleep, may your legacy be honored for generations to come, may the tears shed over your coffins fertilize the fields of patriotism in our nation to raise a new generation built on strength and honor, able and willing to follow in your footsteps when duty call to defend America. May your blood not have been shed in vain. May we prove worthy of your sacrifice. May we always honor your parents so they will always know that they are the parents of an American hero.

You are our brave ones, our heroes, and our national treasures. You are the pride of our nation, our strength and our foundation. Thanks to you, millions have been freed around the world. Thanks to you, those who criticize our country, burn our precious flag, and speak ill of you, are able to do so because their freedom is built upon your blood and your sacrifice.

I salute you one and all. I bow before you in respect and humility. May God bless you and bless America, land of the free and home of the brave, and the dream that became my address." Well said Brigette, and welcome to our great country. You are a true American Patriot.

America's Public Enemy #1

I know I mentioned this in chapter seven, but it has to go in this chapter as well. As our boys from Navy SEAL team six, just down the street from me in Dam Neck, Virginia pulled off a deadly mission no one thought possible after a ten year man-hunt of Osama bin Laden. Fabled SEAL team six officially doesn't exist, crew members usually only last about three years on the team due to burn out and the fact that they are usually gone 300 days out of a year.

The successful bin Laden mission was a much needed boost for the unit. The unit's reputation took a hit in 2010 after a rescue mission took the life of a British hostage, where one member of the unit was released. This was also the same unit that rescued American Richard Philips a captain of a small ship from Somali pirates in 2009, killing three of the four pirates.

Our armed forces do the most selfless and dangerous work there is, for the most noble and vital cause there is, and they do it for you and me. They expose themselves to unimaginable horrors without asking for recognition or praise. They carry out orders without question or complaint. Their experiences provide them with a perspective on the costs and value of freedom that the rest of us rarely, if ever experience. I think that's something that every American should give thanks for, whenever we're given the chance. This is definitely the last best place on earth, and we must all be committed to defending her to the end, in some way or another. I would like to share a piece with you that is still being read at most Navy retirement ceremonies. Its call "The Watch" and it goes like this (and it still gives me goose bumps):

The Watch

For twenty years this sailor has stood the watch
While some of us were in our bunks at night,
This sailor stood the watch
Yes…even before some of us were born into this world,
This shipmate stood the watch
Many times he would cast an eye ashore and see his family standing there,
Needing his guidance and help,
Needing that hand to hold during these hard times,
But he still stood the watch
He stood the watch for twenty years,
He stood the watch so that our families,

And our fellow countrymen could sleep soundly in safety,
Each and every night, knowing that a sailor stood the watch
Today we are here to say:
Shipmate…the watch stands relieved
Relieved by those you trained, guided, and lead
Shipmate you stand relieved…we have the watch!

Ronald A. Martin Jr.

Blogs in relation to this Chapter (We the People have Spoken)

- Not until I moved to a city with a huge military presence did I realize the sacrifice the military families make. You see it in the faces of the spouses and the children as they valiantly roll with whatever comes their way.

- I have the best income stream you could have. A retired military pension and health care for life. Oh yea, I started collecting it at age 37! I'm amazed at our misguided youth who do not consider the military as an option.

- When my son joined the Army I asked him why he wanted to join and he answered "my country is at war and if I don't do my part than I will have no honor." Thank God for those young people who still believe in doing what is needed with courage and honor.

- Service members work harder than any other employee government or private that you can find. The average service member makes $33k a year, and unless they decide to stay 20 or more years they do not get a pension. They also deploy away from their families every other year and put their own lives on the line for our country that no longer appreciates them. We are a pathetic country for bitching about salaries and don't even think about cutting entitlement programs that are enablers of laziness. Wake Up America!!!!

-Thank you for your sacrifices. I'm sorry I never noticed before, We all should have.

-It's a shame for the Vet and their families. For all that they go through they are the first place government looks to get pay and benefits cut.

-For all the homeless Vets…get your butts out of the country and find work elsewhere. Those of is with small government pensions can afford *to live hundreds of places outside the United States comfortably. I have been doing it for seven years now.*

-I agree that every single American is worried about the far reaching hands of the radical Islamist groups. However, the US military stares them in the face daily and their families are left to worry every time the phone rings. Every military spouse will live in fear until their military member comes homes.

VII

Possible signs of Recovery

"The ultimate measure of a man is not where he stands in moments of comfort and convenience, but where he stands at times of challenge and controversy."
-Martin Luther King, Jr.
"When governments fear people, there is liberty. When the people fear the government, there is tyranny."
-Thomas Jefferson

I have made this one of the last chapters for a reason. It may very well be the shortest chapter in this book, as I wait until the last possible minute to hope, experience, and write about positive signs before this book goes to the presses. So here goes...

On November 02, 2010 the Republicans won the House of Representatives, reflecting Americans anxiety about their livelihoods and anger about the economy and high unemployment.

The result was the House's biggest turnover in 70 years. Republicans pledged that they will use their new role to seek a smaller, less costly, and more accountable government. Wasting no time, on December 2, 2010, House republicans plan to eliminate a global warming committee created by democrats. Republican and soon to be Speaker of the House John Boehner, said disbanding the panel is part of the republican pledge to cut waste in the government and this process will save several million dollars. I guess that's a start, but let's look deeper into the issue. There are currently sixty four federal departments and or agencies in play right now that count for 2,112 subsidy programs. The federal government is dispensing hundreds of billions of dollars annually to state government, businesses, non-profit groups, and individuals. Here is an example: (See figure 3)

Dept. or Agency	Subsidies	Dept. or Agency	Subsidies
Agriculture	229	Interior	217
Commerce	96	Homeland Security	96
Defense	66	Housing Urban Dev.	117
Education	170	Justice	125
Energy	37	Labor	62
Health Human	419	State	25
Treasury	11	Veterans Affairs	44
EPA	109	Small Business	24
Transportation	84	All Others	237

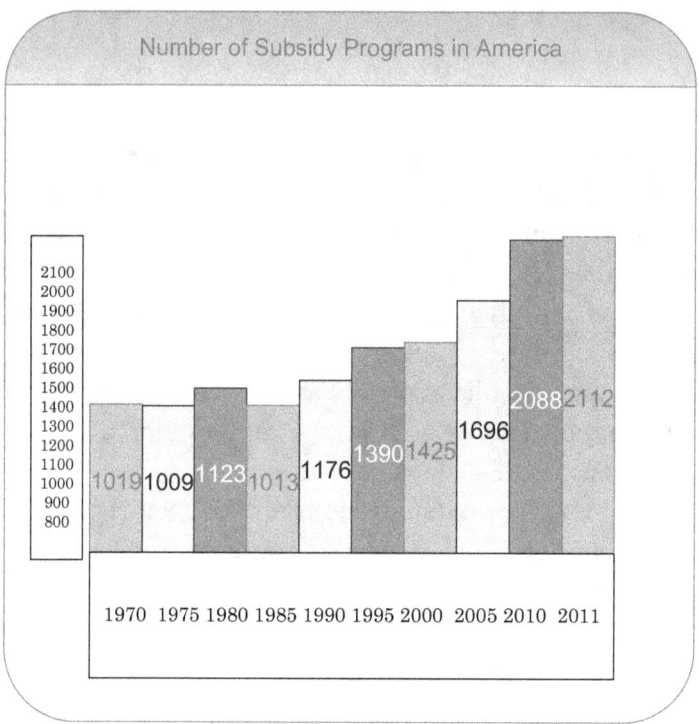

Figure 3

The Catalog of Federal Domestic Assistance (CFDA) provides an official listing of all federal aid (or subsidy) programs, including grants, loans, insurance, scholarships, and many other types of cash and non-cash benefits. Here is an example of 10 of the newest programs added to the CFDA. Each new subsidy programs comes with complex rules regarding eligibility, funding formulas, reporting requirements, auditing and so forth.

Healthy marriage promotion	150,000,000
Safety belt performance grants	124,500,000
Incentive fund to raise teacher's pay	99,000,000
Prisoner re-entry job search help	21,000,000
Clean fuels program for city buses	17,600,000
Specialty crop block grant	7,000,000
Motorcycle safety education grants	6,000,000
Environmental justice training grants	1,000,000

Museum professionals training grants   982,000
Steps to healthier girls   60,000

Hey John Boehner, I have an idea on how to save about 400 million dollars….. On September 08, 2010 the federal government implemented a traveler's tax. Traveler's flying to the states from certain countries will be required to pay a fourteen dollar "operational and travel promotion fee" if they do not possess a United States visa. The fee affects air and sea travelers from about thirty seven countries presently.

<u>Cracking Down on Border Security</u>

Since the 2004 "Southwest Border Security Bill", the border patrol has doubled in size to over twenty thousand agents. The National Guard has been given authorization to deploy up to an additional twelve hundred troops to the border until Customs and Border Protection (CBP) can recruit and train more agents to serve on the border. Immigration and Customs Enforcement (ICE) special agents have tripled to focus on cartel violence along the southwest border: CBP and ICE have seized more than 103 million dollars in illegal currency, more than 1.7 million dollars in kilograms of drugs and more than 1,400 firearms.

Project Deliverance resulted in more than 2,200 arrests, seizure of 74 tons of drugs and 154 million dollars in U.S. currency. Project Coronado resulted in 303 arrests and seizure of 3.4 million dollars in U.S. currency, 729 pounds of meth, and 62 kilos of cocaine, 967 pounds of marijuana, 144 weapons, and 109 vehicles. Operation Xcellerator resulted in 750 arrests and seizure of more than 23 tons of narcotics and 59 million in U.S. currency. Statistics reflect a significant reduction in the number of people attempting to cross the U.S. border illegally. CBP statistics show illegal immigration into the United States is down. It can be done. If we secure the border, deport the criminals, sanction employers who hire illegals, deny citizenship and social welfare except emergency aid, in five to ten years our crisis would be at end. If we don't do this, the crisis will end America.

A jump in Immigration prosecutions?

New government data shows the Obama administration has sharply increased immigration prosecutions and has stepped up the cases against white-collar crimes, drug violations, organized crime and official corruption. Transactional Records Access Clearinghouse (TRAC), a private, nonpartisan group based at Syracuse University has compiled data from the first two years of the Obama administration and the last two years of the Bush administration. TRAC said that felony immigration prosecutions in the federal court systems along the border from Houston to San Diego went up 259% from 2007 – 2010, increasing nearly 16,000 – 36,210.

Cracking down on Radical Islamist?

Tennessee is considering making it a felony to follow the Islamic code known as Shariah, the most severe measure yet put forth by a national movement whose members believe extremist Muslims want Shariah to supersede the U.S. Constitution. The legislation simply states that Shariah follows the laws of jihad, which calls for the violent overthrow of Tennessee and the U.S. government is the issue at hand and it must be stopped.

A hidden document was found seven years ago on how America's Constitution will be replaced by Shariah law. The document was written well before 9/11 and the strategy seemed to be too outlandish to be taken seriously. But by failing to take it seriously allowed the Islamist strategy to gain traction, with the first signs of its success already visible. According to the non-partisan report, The Islamist document calls for the strategy plan to be slowly implemented in phases that enable Shariah to "creep" into US culture. To work, it requires Muslims to gain influence in various ways including: expanding Muslim's physical presence here in the US via high birth rates, immigration (legal/illegal) and refusing to assimilate; keeping Americans "in the dark" over human rights infringement by ensuring they do no study Shariah doctrine and its impact.

The good news of this article is that Americans and some States are finally waking up to these issues. But we need our leadership to take it seriously also before it's too late. As of the writing of this book the Obama administration has yet to do anything about these reports out of a ridiculous concern that mentioning an Islamic link will offend moderates.

Generous Tax Breaks?

President Obama and key law makers from both political parties say it's time for a serious national discussion about making the tax code simpler and fairer. It's going to be a long talk and one that could last years. Republican Dave Camp, R-Mich says "To really reform the tax code in a way that lowers the tax rate, broadens the base and promotes the competitiveness of American companies is not going to be an easy task." Camp also said that the tax code is 10 times the size of the Bible, with none of the good news. Obama has reportedly said he wants to simplify the tax code by broadening the tax base and lowering the tax rates. That means reducing the number of credits, deductions, and exemptions – for businesses and individuals.

Secretary of Defense Robert Gates has been on a recent tear doing what he feels is best for our country in his attempt to save around one billion dollars. So as it has been done in the past the first place they start looking is at the military.

House votes to end subsidies for Candidates

On 26 January 201, the Republican controlled house voted to end multi-million dollar federal subsidies for Presidential candidates and national political conventions. The first of what party leaders promised to be weekly, bite-sized bills to attack record deficits.

Eliminating this program would save tax payers about 617 million dollars over ten years, and would require candidates and political parties to rely on private contributions rather than tax dollars.

Private Sectors are more Confident about Hiring?

After three years of cutbacks, furloughs, and wage freezes, the outlook for American workers is improving. Workers will receive the largest pay increase this year since the start of the "Great Recession". Merit-based pay increases are expected to average 3% this year, up from 2.7% in 2010, but still shy of the average 3.5% before the recession. The findings were based on a survey of about four hundred large and mid-size employers conducted in January and February.

In addition, most companies have lifted the salary freezes they implemented during the recession. Only 5% of companies that froze salaries in 2010 are planning to continue the freezes in 2011. The survey's finding reflect growing confidence among employers will add 2.4 million jobs this year (2011), double the 950 thousand jobs added in 2010. This will still fall short of the 8.3 million jobs lost during the recession, most of which will never be coming back. It's not great but it is a start.......

Bill would limit citizenship by birth

Four republicans are attempting to limit automatic citizenship for children born in the United States to illegal immigrants. Senator David Vitter, R-La., introduced legislation that would end what he calls "birth tourism." The measure which faces an uphill battle in the Democratic led Senate, would limit birthright citizenship to children born in the United States who have at least one parent who is a U.S. citizen, legal resident, or active member of the military. GOP Senators Jerry Moran of Kansas, Mike Lee of Utah, and Rand Paul of Kentucky has joined David Vitter in this fight.

Sen. Harry Reid, who is now the Senate majority leader, blasted the rise in what amounts to legal/illegal immigration because of the stress it places on the system. He says, "If you break our laws by entering this country without permission and give birth to a child, we reward that child with U.S. citizenship and guarantee a full access to all public and social services this society provides. And that's a lot of services." The main problem is according to a 2010 nationwide poll by the Pew Research Center for the People and the Press, a majority of Americans –56% opposed changing the 14th Amendment; 41% favored changing it; the remaining 3% did not care one way or the other.

We Finally Got Him!

Osama bin Laden, the face of global terrorism and the architect of the 9/11 attacks was killed in a firefight with the Navy SEALS on Monday 2 May 2011. "Justice has been done" President Barack Obama said in a dramatic announcement at the White House. The military operation took mere minutes, and there were no US casualties. Navy SEALs dropped in from US helicopters at bin Laden's hideout in Pakistan and shot him in the head twice. Three adult males and a female being used as a human shield were also killed in the raid.

America's Public enemy #1 was finally found and dealt with; this story was so big that it made front-page headlines of over 719 newspapers world-wide. Why does it matter so much? It matters because most people had begun to doubt whether American power was truly fading. Most of all, it matters because we have other difficult, long-range problems to solve, and we are running out of role models. The fact that the country can fix a bulls-eye on a difficult target and stay the course and win when no one expected it is a huge accomplishment. President Obama ended his speech with, "We can do things that we set our minds on not because of our wealth or our power, but because of who we are: one nation, under God, indivisible, with liberty and justice for all."

These events had little effect on the US economy. Stocks rose, oil came down a dollar or two, and the dollar got a little stronger. But amid fears of a possible Al-Qaeda retaliation, US security forces remain on high alert, so prices went back to normal the following day.

Possibly trimming some Entitlements to save Money?

Congress is under pressure to cut the rapidly rising costs of the federal government's food stamps program at a time when a record number of Americans are relying on it. The House Appropriations Committee today (31 May 2011) will review the fiscal year 2012 appropriations bill for the Department of Agriculture that includes $71 billion dollars for the agency's "Supplemental Nutrition Assistance Program (SNAP)." That's $2 billion dollars less than what President Obama requested but a 9% increase from 2011, which critics say is too large given the sizeable budget deficit.

A record number of Americans - -about 14 percent or 1 in 7 — now rely on the federal government's food stamp program and its rapid expansion in recent years has become a politically explosive topic. More than 44.5 million Americans received SNAP benefits in March, an 11 percent increase from one year ago and nearly 61 percent higher than the same time four years ago. So when this entitlement was established in 1964, to help people to get on their feet, 21 million households are relying on this entitlement to feed their families. And since there are so many families and individuals on food stamps the program cost taxpayers more than $68 billion dollars last year alone.

The appropriation of money by Congress has never solved poverty or the resulting problems of poverty. It is what I like to call a band-aid effect. Even the Bible says you can give a man a fish and feed him for a day or you can teach him to fish and he can feed himself the rest of his life. The Republican's propose to change the program from an entitlement to a block-grant program tailored for each individual state, much like the proposal for Medicaid. States would no longer receive open-ended subsidies and the aid would be contingent on work or job training. It would also limit funding for the program.

But the President's 2012 budget goes completely in the opposite direction. It aims to make requirements less stringent for certain age groups without dependents. The President also suggested restoring benefit cuts that were included in the Child Nutrition Reauthorization bill last year. So as usual we have one group pulling one way and the other group pulling the other with the ring leader giving the extra tug. I will say it one more time, get off the couch and vote in 2012!

Final thoughts

As always every time a positive sign appears, one or two negative signs show up with or after it. Stocks, gold, and silver are rising, but so is oil/gas, and food. One month unemployment goes down nationally, but up in 25 states. Companies start hiring in some sectors, but lay off thousands in another, we may have to face the music as this being the norm from here on out. But I still say we have time to make a difference if we act now. I cannot stress the importance of every American tax-payer to get out and vote during the upcoming 2012 elections. The next chapter should help guide you through your voting process. You can see the panic in most Americans faces now and we have to do our part to wake up the other percentage that doesn't care or just totally oblivious to what is going on around them.

I will use the example of Donald Trump and his persistency on President Barack Obama's birth certificate issues accomplishes success. He was loud, he was public, and he didn't back down and he finally persuaded Mr. Obama to produce the long awaited birth certificate. I'm not saying that DT is going to be my candidate, he needs more work and I really do not want to see his candidacy in a reality show perspective. But if we can all be that passionate, vocal, and persuasive on all the issues that bother us, this would be a better country by far.

Blogs in relation to this Chapter (We the People have Spoken)

-*Moving from "welfare" to a "jobs" economy would be the first big reality to improving the deficit. Our system of government and handouts encourages too much dependency. It's not in human nature to not be productive*

- *I'm all for tax reform as long as it's not political-speak for Tax Increase.*

- *As usual we are a reactive not proactive country and won't do anything until we have no choice. We have allowed the politicians and law makers convolute our lives to the point that we have no control over anything and in frustration we blame each other. Seems like I remember another similar scenario like this and it was called the Roman Empire.*

- *Bottom line is people willingly sneak into the United States to bear children and it's not just from the Latin countries, it's from all over the world. It's long overdue that we amend the grossly abused 14th amendment. America is not the dumping ground for the world.*

  I'm tired of hearing the only true Americans were the Indians. This is modern America and we have guidelines and laws everyone needs to follow. Everyone that is born here legally is an American. The argument is the illegals coming over here by the millions abusing the system with all the instant entitlements they receive, America is trying to recover and this is a huge burden.

VIII

The Candidates

"There is no medicine like hope, no incentive so great, and no tonic
so powerful as expectation of something tomorrow."
-Orison Swett Marden
"Great hope makes great men."
-Thomas Fuller

As the 57th quadrennial United States Presidential Election quickly approaches us, the question remains of who will be running and can anyone make President Obama a one term President. The 2012 election is likely to be decisively important for the future of our country - -but worrying about Election Day won't make it arrive any sooner. All we can do is let the candidates run who decide to run, urge them to be bold and forth right in laying out their plans for the country, and sit back and enjoy the show.

As the candidates slowly reveal themselves I will attempt to list all potential candidates with a write-up on each one. This will make your job easier in making your determination of who you will be voting for on Nov 6, 2012. Because I know that everyone reading this book will exercise their God given right as an American to be at the polls on that day. If you do not get out and vote that day, you have no right to criticize, bad mouth, and/or complain how this country is ran after that day. And above all you should be ashamed of yourself.

The President

Barack Obama (Current President of the United States) - Judging from history, Barack Obama will most certainly win the nomination of his Democratic Party in 2012, however it is not necessarily a given. We expect to see Democratic candidates take on Obama and announce their candidacy for the 2012 nomination. Persons entering on the Democratic side would be looking more to gain experience and recognition than the nomination of the Party. Ultimately the prospect of a second Obama term depends on his accomplishments over the next two years in the eyes of the American people. The economy (crappy), unemployment (crappy), health care, and other issues of the day are among hundreds of national and international issues upon which Barack Obama will be judged in 2012. You should already know where he stands on the current issues and what he has done about them so far. You should also be well aware of the:

The Stimulus Package

The big question is did Obama's $800 billion stimulus package that Congress passed in the winter of 2009 work? The Congressional Budget Office estimates that it reduced unemployment by somewhere between 0.8 and 1.7 percent and economists say it boosted the G.D.P. by more than two percent. Politically, however, none of this has made any difference. Polls show that a sizable majority of the voters think that the stimulus did nothing to help or hurt the economy, and the consensus is that most Americans oppose any new stimulus plans. Many voters say the stimulus helped the banking sector and the auto industry. If you are or were part of the fifteen million unemployed the stimulus did extend unemployment benefits up to 99 weeks. The plan also may end up transforming things like clean-energy industry, broadband access, the country's infrastructure, and the national power grid, but it's still hard for voters to find concrete evidence of what the stimulus package really has done, but increase the national deficit. So it's not surprising that the voters view is; "We spent $800 billion and all I got was this lousy T-shirt."

The Democratic Challenger?

Hillary Clinton (Secretary of State) – Hillary abruptly announced that she would not serve in a second Obama administration. Is that because she intends to pursue a Clinton administration in 2012? Her announcement comes amid the violence and turmoil in Libya in which the United States, Britain, and France have begun massive air strikes to end Col. Gaddafi's brutal repression of opposition protesters. It's rare for an active member of a sitting President's party to challenge him in the primaries for the nomination. In fact the last time it was done was 1968 when Minnesota Senator Eugene McCarthy took on a weakened Lyndon B. Johnson.

But the Clinton's are not your typical passive politicians. Hillary and her rock star hubby Bill would like nothing more than be back in the White House. Most of us already knew there were three parties; The Republicans, the Democrats, and the Clintons. And if just for a second, they smell Obama's vulnerability and potential defeat by the GOP possible, don't be surprised if she pulls a McCarthy. It's a long shot, but these days in politics anything can and possibly will happen.

The Front Runners

Mitt Romney (Former Gov. of Massachusetts) – Mitt Romney is considered by many as the Republican Party front runner for 2012. Romney a Harvard graduate and longtime venture capitalist is revered for his financial knowledge. Many believe that his financial knowledge can help the struggling US economy a great deal.

Abortion - Mitt Romney states that his views against abortion have evolved and deepened since he took office. He said he would be delighted to sign a federal ban on all abortions if it was passed by Congress. He believes that abortion must be banned except in cases like rape, incest, or in order to save the life of the mother.

Budget - Mitt Romney believes in the principles of reaganomics wherein you cut taxes which is believed to bring economic growth to the country. He believes the budget should cut taxes on people earning incomes less than $200k a year and also cut payroll taxes on Americans aged 65 or older.

Economy - Romney said that America is going through extraordinary times and a well-crafted stimulus plan is needed to put people back to work (not another stimulus). He thinks that any new spending should be limited to projects that are essential and which bring an immediate positive impact. Once the economy is revived he suggest gaining control over the federal budget and also on over entitlement spending on Social security and Medicare. Romney believes only private sector entrepreneurs can create the millions of jobs that the country needs.

Immigration - Romney opposes amnesty or permanent legalization for illegal immigrants and temporary legalization for illegal immigrants as guest workers. He opposes allowing illegal immigrants to getting drivers licenses. Mitt believes that all illegal immigrants should go home eventually and sign up for permanent citizenship legally within a set period of time. With regard to employers who have and are employing illegal immigrants,

Romney feels that if caught they should be subject to sanctions similar to those for not paying taxes in this country. Romney does not support the "Anchor Baby" policy, saying that applicants will have to continue to wait their turn to unite with their loved ones.
Gun Control - Romney has been taking stands both against and in favor of the gun control issue. Initially the governor was on the side of strong gun laws. Just recently he reveals that he is a member of the NRA and owns a gun himself. Even though there is no license issued in his name in the four states he lived.

Newt Gingrich (Former House Speaker) – Newt has thrown his hat into the ring for 2012. Mr. Gingrich is clearly qualified for the position of the President of the United States and is viewed as insightful and shrewd, issue-oriented conservative. He served 20 years in the U.S. House of Representatives and stepped down in 1999. Gingrich recently stated "we have a lot of people around the country who would like to have somebody who represents a commitment to replace the current failed programs and to develop a set of solutions that are practical and workable.
Abortion – Gingrich is a pro-life candidate, he believes that abortion should not be legal. He also believes that anti-abortion laws should focus on punishing the doctors performing the operation and not the mothers who seek it.
Budget – Gingrich thinks the U.S. must quit spending beyond its means. He believes that the budget must be balanced, and Congress must stop spending on discretionary items such as entitlement programs. He said the country could cut costs in half and reduce the deficit by drastically downsizing the government.
Economy – Newt believes our economy has been on a long slide downward that was preventable. He would provide incentives to businesses to create jobs and raise wages, while lowering taxes will keep business here, bring back those who went overseas and provide jobs in the United States economy. He thinks that the liberal coalition keeps complaining about outsourcing jobs but insists on crippling corporate taxes.

Immigration – Gingrich believes that our open borders are a direct threat to our security. He thinks the terrorists can cross our borders at will with little deterrence. He supports the guest worker program, supports tougher restrictions on obtaining worker visas. Gingrich thinks everyone here illegally must go home and apply for legal status - -anything else is amnesty.

Gun Control – Newt believes that every individual has the right to own firearms according to the Constitution and that should not be redefined by nit picking.

Mike Huckabee (Former Governor of Arkansas) Mike is the perfect example of what a conservative Republican should stand for. Huckabee is leading amongst Republicans and has the strongest showing when matched against Barack Obama. But right now Mike seems to be happy spreading his word through the national platform on Fox News.

Abortion – Mike is against abortion as he strongly feels that life starts in the womb. He stated that he would support and be willing to lead a Human Life Amendment to the Constitution. He supports defunding of Planned Parenthood. He also believes that life is a gift from God and we have no right to end it.

Budget – Mike supports the elimination of federal income and payroll taxes. Huckabee claims that he steered Arkansas from a $200 million deficit to an $850 million surplus. He thinks' Obama's Health care bill is no more than redistribution of wealth. If elected Mike said he would not support the raising of income taxes at the Federal Level, he supports the abolition of the death tax and supports fair tax of 23% tax on consumption. Huckabee would maintain long-term solvency of Social Security and Medicare.

Economy – Mike proposes various tax cuts and finally abolishing the income tax with sales tax. Huckabee would increase the usage of wind power and decrease dependence on foreign oil. He would extend rebate to all purchases made below the poverty line so that the poor are not taxed. He supports flat tax, globalization and line item veto power believing that the line item veto power will help curb spending. Mike also supports free trade to rake in more

revenue but insists it has to be fair trade. Huckabee advocates reigning in and out of control spending to balance the budget.
Immigration – Mike opposes driver's licenses for illegal immigrants. He opines that illegal immigrants should go home and start over again. He feels that the country owes this priority to the legal immigrants who have been waiting in line for a long time. Huckabee proposed building a border fence within the first 18 months of taking office. He says by doing this there would be no open door for people to just walk in and out of at will. Mike supports the training and deployment of 23,000 more law enforcement personnel, erect 105 radar and camera towers and build 700 miles of border fence. Huckabee also acknowledges America's need for doctors and engineers in abundance but says they should enter the country legally.
Gun Control – Mike strongly supports the right to bear arms and opposes restrictions on access to firearms. He says while he doesn't consider himself to be a "gun nut", he proudly owns a variety of firearms and enjoys hunting as well as sports shooting. He believes Americans have the right to own firearms for self-protection and as a matter of principle. Huckabee supports the "Castle Doctrine" which is a person's right to stand his/her ground and meet force with force. Huckabee added "I think it's the way it ought to be. We have the right to protect ourselves."

Ron Paul (U.S. Representative from Texas) His main source of support is the recently formed TEA Party which shares his views that government should be smaller and less intrusive. He has vowed never to vote for any legislation that is quite volatile in the political climate. Paul believes that the income tax should be abolished and thinks that the country would benefit from the absence of nearly all government agencies, maintaining that they waste incredible amounts of tax dollars while accomplishing very little.
Abortion – Ron is Pro Life and has delivered more than 4,000 babies during his career as an obstetrician. Paul says abortion is murder and protecting the unborn is protecting liberty. Paul thinks there

should be no federal funding of abortion and no tax funding for organizations that promote abortion.

Budget – Paul Believes that nations and empires inevitably end due to financial reasons. He believes that the U.S. should live within its means and pay down the deficit. He thinks spending should be based on the Constitution. If all spending had to be justified by the Constitution our spending would be drastically reduced. Paul says we cannot afford the wars in the Middle East. He doesn't believe that government should bail out private enterprise nor seek to control it. Ron supports a Balanced Budget Amendment and on-budget accounting.

Economy – Ron believes the economy will improve when the government stops interfering in business matters. Business should not be curtailed by excessive government regulations. He also believes that stimulus doesn't work.

Immigration – Paul believes immigrants should be dealt with economically; we are in worse shape now because we subsidize immigration, and when you subsidize something you have more of it. He believes we should amend the Constitution to remove alien's birthright citizenship. Paul doesn't believe in amnesty, but thinks it's impractical to round up 15 – 30 million illegal immigrants and ship them back. He feels we should end all incentives and amnesty for illegal immigration.

Gun Control – Paul supports the Second Amendment and believes law-abiding citizens should be able to carry concealed firearms that are legally owned and registered. Ron believes all bans and measures that restrict law-abiding citizens from owning legally obtained firearms should be repealed. He believes that government should ease procedures on the purchase and registration of firearms. Paul also scored an A by NRA on pro-gun rights policies.

Tim Pawlenty (Current Gov. of Minnesota) – He didn't seek a third term as Governor of Minnesota, leading to speculation that he's considering a potential bid for 2012. Pawlenty, who had been considered a leading candidate for vice presidential nomination with McCain in 2008, has been making his political rounds.

Abortion – Tim is pro-life and a strong supporter of pro-life issues. He believes there is no greater liberty than the right to life and that should be extended to the unborn. He also believes there should be a twenty four hour waiting period before women can decide on abortion.

Budget – Pawlenty supports the federal spending freeze. He would establish foreclosure assistance hotlines and counseling. He thinks politicians make the budget hard to understand on purpose to gain political advantage. Pawlenty also thinks there should be a balanced budget amendment, the first step in getting spending under control.

Economy – Pawlenty thinks the federal government should be responsible for the financial health of private companies. He thinks that banks should have been allowed to fail. Tim believes that the auto industry should have filed for bankruptcy. He also stated that the stimulus was too big and it was, for the most part, ineffective.

Immigration – Pawlenty is a staunch advocate of border control. He thinks that federal verification of citizenship or legal immigration status should be required for state employment. He thinks that state and local law enforcement should be allowed to work with ICE and other federal law enforcement officials regarding illegal immigration. Tim thinks illegal immigration should be deported whether or not they have committed a crime other than unlawfully entering the country. He thinks our borders should be closed, guarded and open only to immigrants or visitors who are entering the country legally.

Gun Control – Pawlenty supports the Second Amendment. He supports training and background checks for citizens to carry firearms. He also believes in a relentless and aggressive crack down on illegal gun ownership.

Gary Johnson (Former Gov. of New Mexico) – Gary, the former two-term Governor of New Mexico, announced his entry into the Republican nomination race for the 2012 Presidential Election on April 21, 2011. The 58-year old construction company owner has decided to bypass the presidential exploratory phase and is centering his campaign on the promise of "fixing the mess" that the government got us in.

Abortion – Despite being an anti-abortionist on a personal level, Johnson believes that the final decision should be left to the woman herself. However, he is supportive of legislations that require parental consent in cases involving minors.

Budget – Gary has been quoted as saying that the country is 'essentially bankrupt' and is on the verge of financial collapse, a statement that no one is questioning. He believes that the out of control national debt can only be contained by adopting stringent fiscal policies and getting our troops back home from their expensive excursions in Afghanistan, Iraq, and now Libya. Massive spending cuts, one of the hallmarks of his Governorship of New Mexico, are one of the first steps that need to be taken, along with decentralization of Medicare and Medicaid to individual state control.

Immigration – He is against the current militarized border between the United States and Mexico, and envisions a time when there will be free-flowing traffic between the two countries. He believes that a new legislation on drugs would put a stop to a majority of smuggling activities at the border. Johnson is also of the opinion that controlled immigration is beneficial to the country and dismisses the idea that immigrants are taking away jobs from hard working Americans, citing the fact that most of the jobs being involved are the low paying ones that are less attractive for locals.

Gun Control – Johnson believes in the right of citizens to bear arms and is convinced that outlawing firearms will only leave criminals with access to them, thereby negating the deterrence factor. While he personally does not own a gun, he wants the chance to be left open to him. He feels that current gun control legislation is inadequate and can be improved upon.

Rick Santorum (Former Senator of Pennsylvania) –

Santorum is considered both a Social and fiscal conservative. He is particularly known for his stances on the U.S. invasion of Iraq,

Social Security, intelligent design, homosexuality and illegal immigration. He also believes his confrontational 'in your face' style of politics and government will help him succeed in his 2012 campaign.

Abortion – Rick is pro-life and believes that "a child is a child" and that even if that child was conceived as a result of violence then it is at no fault of the child. Therefore he argues that even in the case of rape and incest abortion should be illegal.

Economy – Rick supports the Paul Ryan budget proposal that would strip $60 billion dollars in spending as an effort to reduce the deficit and reform Medicare and Medicaid. He supports making the Bush tax cuts permanent and that we need to stop punishing people who have worked for their money. He argues that the top wage earners in this country are also the job creators.

Immigration – Rick believes in enforcing current existing immigration laws. He openly opposes amnesty for illegal immigrants and supports the construction of a barrier along the U.S. – Mexican border. Rick also supports an increase in the number of border patrol agents and stationing National Guard troops along the border as well. He believes that undocumented immigrants should be deported immediately and that illegal immigrants should not receive any benefits from the government. Finally, the former senator believes that English should be established as the national language in the United States.

Gun Control – Rick is in support of the Constitutional Amendment that gives citizens the right to bear arms. Santorum as senator voted yes on a bill that bans lawsuits against gun manufacturers in 2005. He also introduced a bill called the Sportsman Privacy Protection Act which would prohibit the government from collecting the social security numbers of gun owners when they sign up for gun licenses.

Mike Bloomberg (Mayor of NYC) – Independent – A self-made millionaire and philanthropist, he has experience in executive management and maintains a largely non-partisan approach to problem solving. He has been a Democrat, a Republican, and now an Independent. He is "liberal" on social issues and "conservative" on fiscal and government concerns. He wants sensible immigration reform while giving amnesty to the illegal immigrants who are already in the country. Bloomberg is a fervent advocate for abortion rights and endorses gay marriage and limited gun control. He would like to see government more involved in "climate change" and public welfare programs. He did, after all balance New York City's budget, a feat that his recent predecessors could not perform. He believes that the nation's infrastructure should be rebuilt, which in turn will yield more revenue and contribute to improving the job market in the coming years aside from the construction jobs it will provide. He also advocates Saturday voting to make it easier for the working Americans to vote.

Abortion - Mayor Bloomberg thinks that women should control their own reproduction. They should have the right of abortion on demand. He also states that reproductive choice is a human right.

Budget - Mayor Bloomberg believes deficit spending is a road to ruin. He asserts that cuts must be made is discretionary spending first before cutting programs aimed at helping the disadvantaged. As a public official whose salary is $1 per year, he believes that public official and Congressional representatives should take pay and benefit cuts to help get the nation's finances back in the black.

Economy - Mayor Bloomberg favors giving tax cuts to businesses to encourage growth and hiring of more workers. He would create incentives for both workers and employers. He would also rebuild infrastructure to spur employment and boost spending, increasing government revenues through income tax.

Immigration - Mayor Bloomberg is in favor of immigration, he stated that New York City would collapse without illegal labor. He believes border control is unrealistic. He thinks that amnesty should be given to those illegal immigrants already in the country. He also thinks that those who do not want to become US citizens should have access to visas that allow them to work in the US.

Gun Control- Mayor Bloomberg believes in the Second Amendment but does not believe criminals should have guns (who does). Along with Boston mayor Thomas Menino, he formed the Mayors against Illegal Guns (MAIG) to make it harder for criminals to get guns. The organization currently has 451 mayors on its roles. He also supports the confiscation of illegally owned guns and guns that are illegal for civilians to own.

Mitch Daniels (Current Gov. of Indiana) – Regarded as a fiscal conservative among his peers and two-term Governor of Indiana and a potential presidential candidate for the Republican Party. Mitch took a nearly $200 million dollar Indiana deficit to a $1.3 billion dollar surplus. His results are even more remarkable considering he actually authorized the lowering of the state's property taxes by 30%, as well as expanding the insurance coverage for an additional 48,000 citizens through the Healthy Indiana Plan. Many have expressed their admiration for his convictions, even calling him "America's Best Governor"

Abortion – Mitch is Pro-life. He maintains that abortion should be legal only if pregnancy results from incest, rape, or life of the mother in danger.

Budget– Mitch believes that it will be painful to fix our federal budget but that we must begin soon. He believes the budget cuts combined with tax increases and privatization plans can help balance the federal budget like it did Indiana's Budget.

Economy – Mitch says that growth friendly tax cuts can reverse economic decline, as it did during his Governorship of Indiana.

Immigration – Mitch believes that immigrants should come here legally. He thinks that the laws should be enforced but he realizes immigrants are vital for businesses. Immigrants should be required to learn English and pay taxes, and illegal immigrants should not be allowed to have drivers' licenses. Daniels believes that businesses cited three times for employing illegal immigrants should lose their license.

Gun Control – Mitch believes gun ownership is a right, where no background checks or licenses should be required. He thinks that everyone should be able to carry concealed weapons.

The Long Shots

Herman Cain (Small Businessman) – Cain, whose resume includes bringing Godfather's Pizza out of near bankruptcy as its CEO, says his business experience can help shape the country. Cain says he would prioritize his strategy as follows: First, he would lower the top corporate tax rate from 35% to 25%. Second, he would make tax rates permanent. Third, Cain proposes lowering the capital gains tax rate to 0%. Fourth, he would tax 0% on repatriated profits - - profits made in a business or investment in a foreign country then brought back to the U.S. Fifth,, he would make a one-year payroll tax holiday of 6.2% for both employees and employers. "I will guarantee that if we did all of those in one bill and put that into law, our economy would grow at least twice the rate it is now," he said.

In addition, Cain is in favor of what has been called a "Fair Tax." Under this kind of tax, federal income tax would be eliminated and instead a consumption-based tax would be imposed. That means people would pay less income tax, but pay higher sales tax on goods and services. He believes that illegal immigration is three problems in one. He says secure the borders, enforce the laws we already have in place, and promote the path to citizenship that is also already in place. Herman ends by saying "Don't condemn me because the first black President was bad," with a big smile on his face.

Abortion – Cain, a devout Christian, has made it very clear that he is against abortion and wants to make it illegal, even in cases of rape.

Budget – Instead of complicated budget trimming exercises, Cain advocates wholesale and decisive major cuts to bring our deficit back to more manageable levels.

Economy – Cain believes a direct stimulus can be created to reinvigorate the economy by simply reducing bureaucratic expenditure and doing away with subsidies for special interest groups.

Gun Control – Cain, despite some vague comments, follows the party line on the issue and supports a citizen's right to bear and keep arms.

Sarah Palin (Former Governor of Alaska) – Sarah gained international recognition upon her selection by John McCain as the 2008 Republican vice presidential nominee. In the past year Palin has become immensely popular among a large portion of the GOP base. In Feb, 2010, Palin said she would run in 2012 "if I believed that that is the right thing to do for our country and the Palin family." She has been weighing in on nearly all Obama initiatives and voicing the opposition at every opportunity. While Palin is no doubt a rising star among Republican conservatives, a recent ABC News/Washington Post poll shows that six in ten Americans view her as unqualified for the job of President in 2012. Nonetheless, Sarah is a force that the Republican Party must reckon with.

Abortion – Palin is opposed to abortion whatever the case, except if the life of the mother was at stake. She says rape victims should be counseled and persuaded to choose life for their babies. She says she is for preventive measures that are legal and safe, but would like to see fewer and fewer abortions in this world.

Budget – Palin has left behind a history of tax cuts as Governor of Alaska. She has made history by bringing forth second largest cuts in the construction budget of the state. She calls for increasing government oversight of investment banks also advocating elimination of federal earmarks and wasteful governmental spending. She criticizes President Obama's spending policies to revive the economy, saying that Americans already have more than $14 trillion in debt and borrowing more would only lead to socialism.

Economy – Palin sought to spur economic growth and thereby increased energy supplies in Alaska while in office as governor by supporting drilling in the Alaska Wildlife National Refuge. Palin says that only with discipline can we foster economic growth and suggested billions of surplus funds to be deposited in state savings. She blames predator lenders for coaxing Americans to live beyond their means. In situations where people could afford to buy a $100k house, they were forced to buy one for $300k. Palin is a firm believer in free market capitalization saying that it encourages best and most competitive projects and ensures a fair democratic process.

Immigration – According to Palin it is not economically possible to deport the 15 – 30 million illegal immigrants. She says that they should be made to follow the rules and made to understand that legal immigrants will have the first preference of opportunities provided by this great country. Not having expressed her views on illegal immigration often, she supports citizenship for the illegal immigrants but feels there should be no amnesty for them. She feels the illegal immigrants require more vocational training, the end of gang violence, assistance to seniors and mostly outreach and communication within their communities.

Gun Control – Palin is a full supporter of the right to keep and bear arms as stated in the Constitution. In her own words, "I am a lifetime member of the NRA, I support our Constitutional right to bear arms and am a proponent of gun safety programs for Alaska's youth." Palin herself has commented that her freezer is full of wild game. Palin supports the campaign to end the ban on handguns and opposes restrictions on access to firearms.

Jon Huntsman (Former Gov. of Utah) – He's relatively young, he's vigorous, he's rich, he's a proven vote getter, he's admired, he's Mormon, and he's scandal free. So what makes Jon Huntsman think he can jump the line and become the GOP's presidential nominee in 2012? Mr. Huntsman's strategy is to emerge as the "maverick" in the Republican race. He has hired the core players from the McCain campaign to help him craft this appeal. Jon is a Republican, with conservative fiscal credentials and a mixture of position on the social issues. I suggest that we all do more research on this candidate as it becomes available to us.

Abortion – Jon is perhaps the most pro-life candidate in the GOP. He has already signed a slew of bills designed to limit or ban abortion altogether.

Economy – Huntsman said he had nothing to do with the shaping of Obama's economic policy – but he does have to deal with its consequences. As the Chinese Ambassador, he saw fiscal policies that deepened the deficit and required billions of dollars in loans from the Chinese government. Jon decided to run based on "in order to project strength abroad, we have to be strong at home." **Gun Control** – As governor, Huntsman signed two bills that loosened Utah's gun regulations. One allowed drivers to keep loaded firearms in their vehicles without a concealed weapons permit, and the other required local businesses to allow cars parked on their property to contain loaded firearms - - or provide secure storage for their customer's guns.

Just in case they throw their hat in the ring

Rick Perry (Governor of Texas) – Rick is a Republican conservative. He is the longest serving current U.S. governor in office to date at 11 years. Governor Perry first said he was not interested in running for president, but his family and supporters have asked him "to give it a second thought" as "our country is in trouble." Perry has drawn attention for his criticism of the Obama administration's handling of the recession, and for turning down approximately $555 million in stimulus money for unemployment insurance. In September 2009, Perry declared that Texas was recession-proof. This is another candidate I would keep an eye on and conduct more research on, if and when he throws his hat in the ring.

Abortion – Governor Perry is the most pro-life governor Texas has ever had, and he has implemented a number of significant reforms to protect life and strengthen Texas families. Rick only believes abortion should be legal only in cases involving rape, incest, or mental health.

Economy – Perry says that the major budget issue will be over the surplus. How much will be dedicated to paying down the national debt, how much to tax cuts, how much to increase defense spending, and whether and how to change key entitlement programs, such as Medicaid, Medicare, and Social Security?

Immigration – Rick says we cannot have homeland security without border security. He says, we need 1,000 National Guard troops to support current law enforcement operations on our border until they can provide 3,000 more border patrol agents that are needed. He believes that Predator drones flying along the borders providing real time Intel for operation centers is also need. Governor Perry believes we should track the citizenship status of those receiving state-funded services so we can get our hands around the financial impact of Washington's failure to handle the immigration challenge. Finally, he is concerned about the large number of deported felons that are returning to the U.S. and filling up the state prisons and local jails.

Gun Control – Rick opposes any restrictions on the right to bear arms. In my opinion, we should all have gun right laws like Texas does. The country would be a much safer place.

Donald Trump (Business Magnate) – Trump is the CEO of Trump Organization, a real estate firm and founder of Trump Entertainment Resorts. He is personally worth over two billion dollars. Trump is seriously considering a run as the Republican presidential candidate in 2012. He says the country is headed for disaster and apparently folks in New Hampshire agree with him, he ranked high on a list of possible candidates when a poll was conducted in that state.

Abortion – Trump is pro-life. He respects the rights of women to make their own choices.

Budget – Trump thinks that if something isn't done soon, we'll have a crash worse than that of 1929. In 1999, he proposed taxing the rich with a one-time 14.25% tax to erase the national debt, which he still thinks is a good idea. Trump also says eliminating debt would boost the economy 35% and income taxes could be lowered.

Economy – Trump believes raising taxes is foolish seeing that the United States is the highest taxed nation in the world. He believes the economy would improve if we charge the countries that we protect.

Immigration – Trump thinks that legal immigration should be difficult and illegal immigration should be impossible. He believes we can't absorb all the illegal immigrants and thinks that they are destroying our economy. He wants to take care of our own people first. We are bankrupting our states with illegal immigrants that take advantage of hospital emergency rooms, entitlement programs, and public education.

Gun Control – Trump generally opposes gun control, he thinks that every law-abiding citizen should have a gun if they want to. He believes assault weapons should be banned, "who needs them except criminals and police?" Trump wants a longer wait time for handguns, rifles, and shotguns. We should be able to tell within 72 hours if a person has a record or mental issues that would prohibit gun ownership.

Chris Christie (Gov. of New Jersey) – As of right now governor Christie says he is not running. But if he does here is where he stands.

Abortion – He is against abortion, but does favor restrictions on abortion such as banning partial-birth abortion, requiring parental notification, and imposing a 24 hour waiting period.

Education – Christie is a strong supporter of the state granting tax credits to parents who send their children to private schools.

Gun Control – Chris supports street and aggressive enforcement of the state's current gun laws.

Michele Bachmann (U.S. House Member from Minnesota) – The Tea Party darling, is renowned for her straight talking and often, controversial stance. Her incredible fund raising ability will come in handy should she decide to run for the presidency. In an ABC news organized New Hampshire straw poll on 22 January 2011, showed Bachmann fifth out of twenty potential Republican presidential candidates. Nevertheless, this will enhance her national image, leading to a more prominent role in Congress.

Jim DeMint (U.S. Senator, South Carolina) – The southern conservative, Tea Party darling, laid out his presidential credentials by saying, "I know exactly what needs to be done, and I know that I probably have the management and leadership to do it."

Scott Brown (U.S. Senator of MA) – Brown is a fresh face, new voice, and a Republican star after his upset in the MA primaries to claim Ted Kennedy's former seat.

Paul Ryan (U.S. Representative for Wisconsin's 1st District) – Paul is another fresh face for the Republican Party and has been ranked among the Party's most influential voices on conservative economic policy. Ryan is the chairman of the House Budget Committee, where he played a prominent public role in drafting and promoting the Republican Party's long-term budget proposal. He introduced the plan, *The Path to Prosperity*, in April 2011 to counter the budget proposal of President Barack Obama.

So there you have it. At the writing of this book this is the most current list of possible candidates that I have come up with. I hope each and every person that reads this book will conduct their own research and exercise their God given right as an American to get to the polls in November 2012 and vote for who you believe is the right candidate. It is also our duty as Americans to hold these politicians accountable for their actions. If they do something you feel is wrong, please don't hesitate to call them on it. By know you should know how to use all the available resources at your fingertips to keep them in check. Don't forget about http://www.ontheissues.org, this website will tell you how each candidate voted on each of the top issues. Good luck and God Bless!

Blogs in relation to this Chapter (We the People have Spoken)

-American politics is becoming more of a joke each day. The problem is, nobody's laughing.

-When did the GOP become a reality show?

-They take my money and send it to 152 out of 182 countries world-wide. Let's start a union to take back our country. Voting does not work and never will.

-Let's pray that the elected officials have the same priorities as we do in saving our country or we will all be doomed!!

-I already have my grab and go kit ready to bail out if Obama gets re-elected. Someone please Save Our Ship!!

Conclusion

I wrote this book as an American patriot pitching in to do his part in the awakening of this country. For that to happen I had to wake up myself and when I did I have been going full-speed ahead ever since. Whether you believe it or not we are all in this together. It doesn't matter what party you support, what color your skin is, what religion you are, or where you come from. There is only one race and it is the human race. All that should matter is if you live in this country you should consider yourself an American. If you are not yet an American citizen and you have made this country your home, you should be making that your top priority. If you are here illegally, then you need to return to your home country and try entering the US legally.

I would like to thank the crew at Sirius Patriot Radio, whom I have been listening to for over two years now in all the great insight and information they provide and for the job they do daily in waking up America. Hopefully the information in this book has helped open your eyes and minds to what is going on and what could happen next. This country is truly in trouble, and if you love her then please do your parts in helping her get back on her feet. The politicians like to pit us against each other whether it is republicans against democrats, conservatives against liberals, or even black against white. Please do not continue to listen to the lies. The true fight at this moment seems to be us (tax-payers) against them (government), and that is not right.

I hope I also made it clear in this book that each vote is crucial. Each American has to do his/her homework as 2012 vastly approaches us. I hope the material in chapter eight will provide you with a great head start in your own research process. Forget about the d or the r in front of the candidate's name. Follow the history of the candidate that you like, the one that says they are going to stand up and fight for what you believe in. They say that one vote doesn't matter and I say that is the biggest lie being told and is repeated before every election (They being the evil and very liberal media). Each and every vote counts and matters. You never waste your vote if you vote with your own conscience. Common sense tells us that supporting the individual of our choice, after having studied his/her position on the issues is never a waste.

I know most of you will ask the question "what can I do?" I can tell you that it will not be easy and the work that each and every one of us must do will be long and hard. The most fundamental tool is communication. The American Revolution would not have been possible if it were not for the simple forms of communication such as letters to the editors and pamphlets. Thomas Paine's pamphlet "Common Sense" set the tone for Americans to get off their butts and take action just before the Revolutionary War.

With technology playing a major role in our daily lives, the internet offers many more ways to get involved. Message boards, blogs, online forums, and even Facebook and Twitter can get people's attention and prompt them to participate in discussions to promote ideas on particular issues and candidates. You can start your own website dedicated to the issues that most concern you. Continuing to educate yourself about the issues and the candidates and passing your knowledge on to your family, friends, and co-workers is another huge part. Have your Congressman or Congresswoman's number programmed in your cell phone. When you are sitting in traffic and a particular issue on the radio or a billboard burns your butt, then call them. Washington records each call and they use these calls to gage what's going on with us.

I along with millions of Americans would like to see term-limits put into place on every politician out there. We have politicians that have been around longer than Fidel Castro, Benito Mussolini, and Adolf Hitler combined. I would also like to see campaign contributions come from the state and only the state that the politician is running in. It is unfair for a candidate in Nevada to have a six hundred thousand dollar campaign when only forty five hundred dollars of it came from Nevada.

I also want to stress the importance of shooters and gun owners to join and become members of the National Rifle Association. There are approximately eight million shooters (growing daily) in this country and less than half of them are members of the strongest organization in the free world when it comes to protecting our second amendment rights. The more members we have the stronger the NRA will be. We need to be strong and to defend our precious Second Amendment, because if the Democrats have their way the Second Amendment will be abolished. Never forget you have a duty not a right to defend yourself and your family. God gave you an amazing gift of life. Never surrender that precious gift. Be prepared to fight for it, it is your duty and right as a free person. Also remember that even if you are not a gun enthusiast, if this right is taken from us, the rest of our rights will follow like a domino effect.

You don't need a panel of judges with politically correct ideologies to give you that right. It is better to be tried by twelve than carried out by six. I highly recommend that come Election Day in 2012 and all the elections there after; we do all we can to get rid of all the politicians who support gun-free zones. Get a gun, learn to use it, and do the right thing. Evil needs to be dealt with, and gun-toting, law-abiding Americans are the ones to do the dealing. When terror does strike it will be your left-wing friend, neighbor, or co-worker that is clinging to the back of your shirt begging and pleading for help.

The American Dream isn't dead yet, but it's struggling to maintain relevance for many of us. Maybe we just need to rethink it, and we will find it is very much alive, only in a different form. We as Americans must become more engaged in public matters, get off the couch, off the fence or what other analogy you want to use, just do it. We must attend to our families, volunteer at our churches and in our communities, and be willing to assist a friend, a neighbor, and yes even strangers from time to time. We must continue to mentor to the youth of this country as our parents and grandparents have done with us.

We can no longer sit on our hands and hope someone else will do something. We have to hold our elected representatives accountable, because if they don't wake up and reverse course, we will no longer recognize the country our founders created. It's up to us – We the People – to sound the alarm. President Ronald Reagan said, *"Freedom is never more than one generation away from extinction. We didn't pass it to our children in the bloodstream. It must be fought for, protected, and handed on for them to do the same, or one day we will spend our sunset years telling our children and our children's children what it was once like in the United States of America where men were free"*. We are fighting a war in America for the very heart and soul of our country. This is truly the last best place on earth. Remember there is power in voting and definitely power in prayer. Pray for America, she needs it!

Please visit my website: www.thechiefsbooks.com often for updates and previews on any of my upcoming works, events, giveaways, and just general knowledge and facts of what is actually going on. Do me one last favor. If you enjoyed this book, and the knowledge inside its contents accomplished the mission of awakening you, then please pass this book along to the ones you care about. God Bless us all!

Recommended Reading List

1. **Ted, White, and Blue**, by Ted Nugent
2. **Liberty and Tyranny,** by Mark Levin
3. **Common Sense**: The Case Against and Out-Of-Control Government, Inspired by Thomas Paine, by Glenn Beck
4. **State of Emergency**: The Third World Invasion and Conquest of America, by Patrick Buchanan
5. **Patriots of the American Revolution**: True Accounts by Great Americans from Ethan Allen to George Rogers Clark, by Richard M. Dorson
6. **The Millionaire Next Door**, by Thomas Stanley and William Danko
7. **They must be Stopped**: Why We Must Defeat Radical Islam and How We Can Do It, by Brigitte Gabriel
8. **The Holy Bible**: King James version, by God

Glossary

af·flu·ent – having a great deal of wealth

Caliphate – refers to the first system of government established in Islam, and represented the political unity of the Muslim.

Consumer price index - An index of the changes in the cost of goods and services to a typical consumer, based on the costs of the same goods and services at a base period. *Abbreviation:* CPI

de·pres·sion - an economic condition characterized by substantial and protracted unemployment, low output and investment, etc; slump

extremist – a person who goes to extremes, especially in political matters. A supporter or advocate of extreme doctrines or practices.

fru·gal – characterized by or reflecting economy in the use of resources.

Generation Y – refers to the population group in the US, born around 1976 – 2000. Sometimes called echo boomers due to the fact that they are the children of the baby boomers

G.O.P. - Grand Old Party (an epithet of the Republican Party since 1880).

Grassroots – of or involving the common people as constituting a fundamental political and economic group

Gross domestic product - The monetary value of all of a nation's goods and services produced within a nation's borders and within a particular period of time, such as a year. It became the official measure of the U.S. economy in 1991. It replaced "gross national product," which covered all goods and services produced by U.S. residents regardless of where they were working.

Ideology – is a set of ideas that constitutes one's goals, expectations, and actions.

Infidel – an unbeliever with respect to a particular religion. A person who does not accept the Islamic faith.

Jihad – a holy war waged on behalf of Islam as a religious duty. A crusade for a principle or belief.

Keynes·i·an - 1st Baron Keynes. 1883--1946, English economist. In *The General Theory of Employment, Interest and Money* (1936) he argued that unemployment was characteristic of an unregulated market economy and therefore to achieve a high level of employment it was necessary for governments to manipulate the overall level of demand through monetary and fiscal policies (including, when appropriate, deficit financing). He helped to found the International Monetary Fund and the World Bank

lay·man – a person who is a non-expert in a given field of knowledge. Layman means "common people".

lob·by·ist – A person who tries to influence legislation on behalf of a special interest.

phi·lan·thro·py – the effort or inclination to increase the well-being of humankind. Love of humankind in general.

pov·er·ty - the state or condition of having little or no money, goods, or means of support; condition of being poor; indigence.

pro·di·gious – extraordinary in size, amount, extent, degree, force, etc.

re·ces·sion – Is a period of slow or negative growth, accompanied by unemployment. Economists define as two consecutive quarters of falling GDP.

rhet·o·ric – the study of the effective use of language. The ability to use language effectively.

ser·vi·tude – slavery or bondage of any kind, political or intellectual.

Sheriah law – the code of law derived from the Koran and from the teachings and example of Mohammed; Sharia is only applicable to Muslims.

Tea Party – is a populist political movement in the U.S. that emerged in 2009 through a series of locally and nationally coordinated protests. The stated purpose of the Tea Party movement has been to stop what it views as wasteful government spending, excessive taxation, and strangulation of what the economy through regulatory bureaucracies.

war·fare - the process of military struggle between two nations or groups of nations; war. Armed conflict between two massed enemies, armies, or the like. Conflict, esp. when vicious and unrelenting, between competitors, political rivals, etc.

xen·o·pho·bi·a- an unreasonable fear or hatred of foreigners or strangers or of that which is foreign or strange.

Notes

This book is based largely on my views and personal experiences. The primary sources for official data are the statistical reports posted on the Internet by the Bureau of Labor Statistics, the Census Bureau, the Congressional Budget Office, Wikipedia, and Yahoo News. The Quotes were mainly taken from *The Book of Positive Quotations*, compiled by John Cook. The *"We the People have Spoken"* have come from various blogs that I have compiled.

One: Higher Education

1. Poll: Best shot at success is pinned on schooling, by Mary Beth Marklein, USA Today January 6, 2011
2. Ted, White and Blue 2008, by Ted Nugent
3. The Biggest threats to universal education in the third world, by Misty, http://www.developmentgoals.com/threats/universal-education.html, retrieved 7 July 2009
4. http://twentysomething.com/inthenews.html, retrieved 9 Sep 2009
5. And the most valuable college degree goes to, by Chris Kyle, Yahoo Education, 19 Apr 2011
6. Transition Assistance Program: Workshop Manual, November 2002 edition

Two: State of the Economy

1. Bad Money 2008, by Kevin Phillips
2. Liberty and Tyranny 2009, by Mark Levin

3. The incredible Shrinking City, by Peter Gorenstein, Daily Tickler

4. The United States has not had a balanced budget since 1957, http://www.geldpress.com/2008/07/us-budget-reporting-deception, retrieved on 5 Mar 2011

5. History of the National Debt, http://www.thenationaldebtcrisis.com/history-of-the-national-debt/ , retrieved 6 April 2011

6. http://en.wikipedia.org/wiki/Immigration_to_the_United_St ates, 11/8/10, retrieved on 05 May 2009

7. Secrets of the Plunge Protection Team, by Michael Edward, 13 May 2004

8. The Plunge Protection Team, by John Mauldin, 5 Apr 2003

9. www.cfda.gov

10. Record number of Americans helped by government safety net, by Rani Luhby, CNN Money, 13 Apr 2011

11. https://www.cfda.gov/?s=main&mode=list&tab=list&tabmod e=list, retrieved on 06 Jul 2010

12. Tax System: Too Complex to be Constitutional? By Jack Hough,

13. http://finance.yahoo.com/taxes/article/111855/tax.system.to.b e.constitional

14. http://realestate.yahoo.com/promo/7-towns-where-land-is-free.html, retrieved on 06 May 2010

15. U.S. citizenship and immigration services, EB-5 Immigrant Investor, http://www.uscis.gov/, retrieved 12 Feb 2011

16. They Must Be Stopped 2008, by Brigitte Gabriel

17. Radical Islam's conquest of America: Welcome to the United States of Arabia, by Jeffrey T. Kuhner, The Washington Times, 05 Aug 2010

Three: Preparing for the Worse

1. Personal Home Defense magazine. Article Home Invasion deter, detect, delay and defend by Paul Markel pgs. 68-69, retrieved 09 Sep 2010

2. Arguing with Idiots: by Glenn Beck, pg 62, 63, 133. 2009

3. 5 Scientific Reasons a Zombie Apocalypse could actually happen, by TE Sloth, David Wong, http://cracked.com/, 29 Oct 2007

4. Avoid Home Invasion – 10 Tips on Avoiding Home Invasion, http://www.livesafely.org/, 10 Oct 2010

5. Real Home Safety, http://realhomesafety.com/, 15 Oct 2010

6. Mega-Disaster Planning, TheCityEdition.com, 2011

7. The Holy Bible, by God, Revelations

8. Shariah law on American Shores, by Meredith Jessup, Townhall Magazine, 25 March 2011

9. U.S. extends Mexico Travel warning over drug mayhem, by Reuters, 25 April 2011

Four: Age Old Question (How do I become rich)

1. The Millionaire Next Door, by Thomas Stanley and William Danko

2. Where Is the Grass Greener? The Economics of Happiness, by Brett & Kate McKay, Money & Career, on Sept 27, 2010

3. Treasury may borrow federal retirement funds in debt emergency, by Sean Reilly, Federal Times, 5 Apr 2011

4. 18 things you should never pay for. Ever., by Len Penzo, Len Penzo Dot Com, 2011

5. Can Money Buy Happiness?, by David Futrelk, Money, 18 July 2006

Five: Politics and Religion

1. On Two Wings 2002, by Michael Novak

2. Shattering the Sacred Myths, Politics and Religion, The Academy of Evolutionary Metaphysics, 2005

http://www.evolutionary-metaphysics.net/rise_of_democracy.html, retrieved on 10 Nov 2010

3. Americans in Poll want Deficit Cut with Entitlements Secured: http://www.newsmax.com/US/poll-deficit-entitlements/2010/12/10/id/379533, retrieved 12 Dec 2010

4. StudentnewsDaily.com: Making sense of current events, http://www.studentnewsdaily.com/other/conservative-vs-liberal-beliefs/, retrieved on 11Nov 2009

5. They Must Be Stopped 2008, by Brigitte Gabriel, pg. 76-77

6. The Pew Forum on Religion and Public Life, 2008 U.S. Religious Landscape Survey, http://religions.pewforum.org/reports

Six: The most Respectable Job in America

1. http://news.yahoo.com/s/csm/20101210/cm_csm/347240, retrieved on 13 Dec 2010

2. http://en.wikipedia.org/wiki/Military_history_of_the_United_States, retrieved on 22 Nov 2010

3. http://www.va.gov/vetdata/, retrieved on 11 July 2010

4. Casualties in Iraq: The Human Cost of Occupation, by Margarett Griffs, http://antiwar.com/casualties, retrieved on 12 Jan 2011

5. Uncle Sam wants you to reach out to help America's military families, by Anna Mulrine, The Christian Science Monitor, 12 April 2011

6. They Must be Stopped, Brigette Gabriel, 2008, pg. 237, 238

7. Fabled SEAL Team 6 ends hunt for bin Laden, by Kimberly Dozier, AP Intelligence Writer, 3 May 2011

Seven: Possible Signs of Recovery

1. Generous tax Breaks make tax reform difficult: by Stephen Ohlemacher, Associated Press,

2. http://new.yahoo.com/s/ap/20110120/ap_on_re_us/us_tax_re form

3. House votes to end subsidies for candidates: by David Espo, Associated Press, 26 Jan 2011

4. http://www.wmctv.com/Global/story.asp?S=14163844, retrieved on 01 Mar 2011

5. Employer Survey reveals plans for salary bumps, by Sandra Block, USA Today, 24 Feb 2011

6. Study finds jump in immigration prosecutions, by Pete Yost, Associated Press, 01 Feb 2011

7. Bill would limit citizenship by birth, by Catalina Camia, USA Today, 06 April 2011

8. After bin Laden: A stronger America, by David Von Drehle, Time, 02 May 2011

9. Family Security Matters, by Lt. Colonel James Zumwalt, USMC (ret), http://www.actforamerica.org

10. Is the next immigration fight over "anchor babies"?, by Ed Hornick, CNN, 28 April 2011

11. TRACImmigration, http://trac.syr.edu/tracreport/bulletins/immigration/monthly jan11/gui/

Eight: The Candidates

1. 2012 Presidential Candidates: Comparing the potential candidates on the issues, http://2012.presidential.candidates.org/Bloomberg/

2. The 2012 Ticket, by William Kristol, The Weekly Standard, 11 April 2011

3. Second Helpings, by James Surowiecki, The New Yorker, Sept 20, 2010

4. Is Hillary Planning a Run at Obama in 2012? By Andy Ostray, Political and Pop culture analyst, 21 Mar 2011

Ronald A. Martin Jr.

ACKNOWLEDGMENTS

I would like to thank my wife Lisa for putting up with me through this effort. I would also like to thank my father-in-law Al who did most of the editing and kept me moving in the right direction during this project. A special thanks to all my family whom I love very much. I hope you all enjoy this book as much as I enjoyed writing it. God Bless us all and God Bless America!

ABOUT AUTHOR

I'm a twenty-two year United States Navy veteran, lifetime NRA member, recruiter, and instructor who lives a very normal Christian life. I have a large family that I love spending as much quality time with as I can. Just like most of you my life is very busy and hectic and it is easy to lose track of what is happening around you. About three years ago I had an awakening and I want to do my job as a great American to awaken as many people as I can with my first book while we still have a fighting chance.